Smarty Kids

Learning Shapes by Coloring

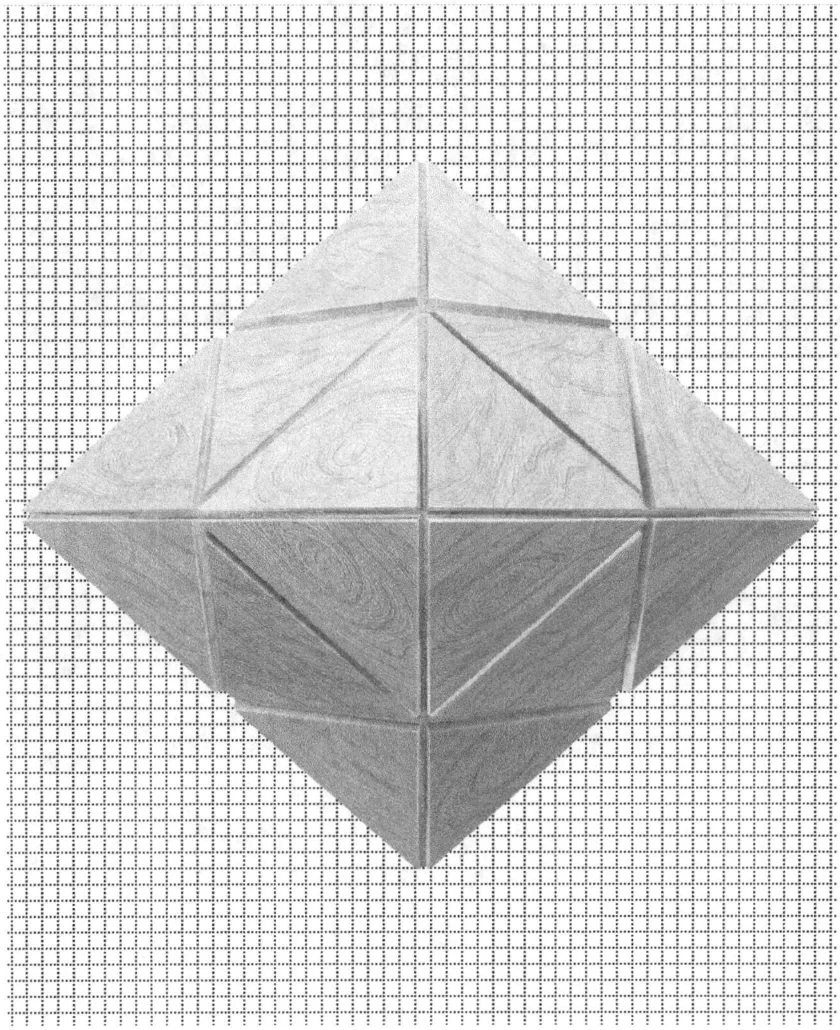

Author: Durollari

Co-Author: Glasner

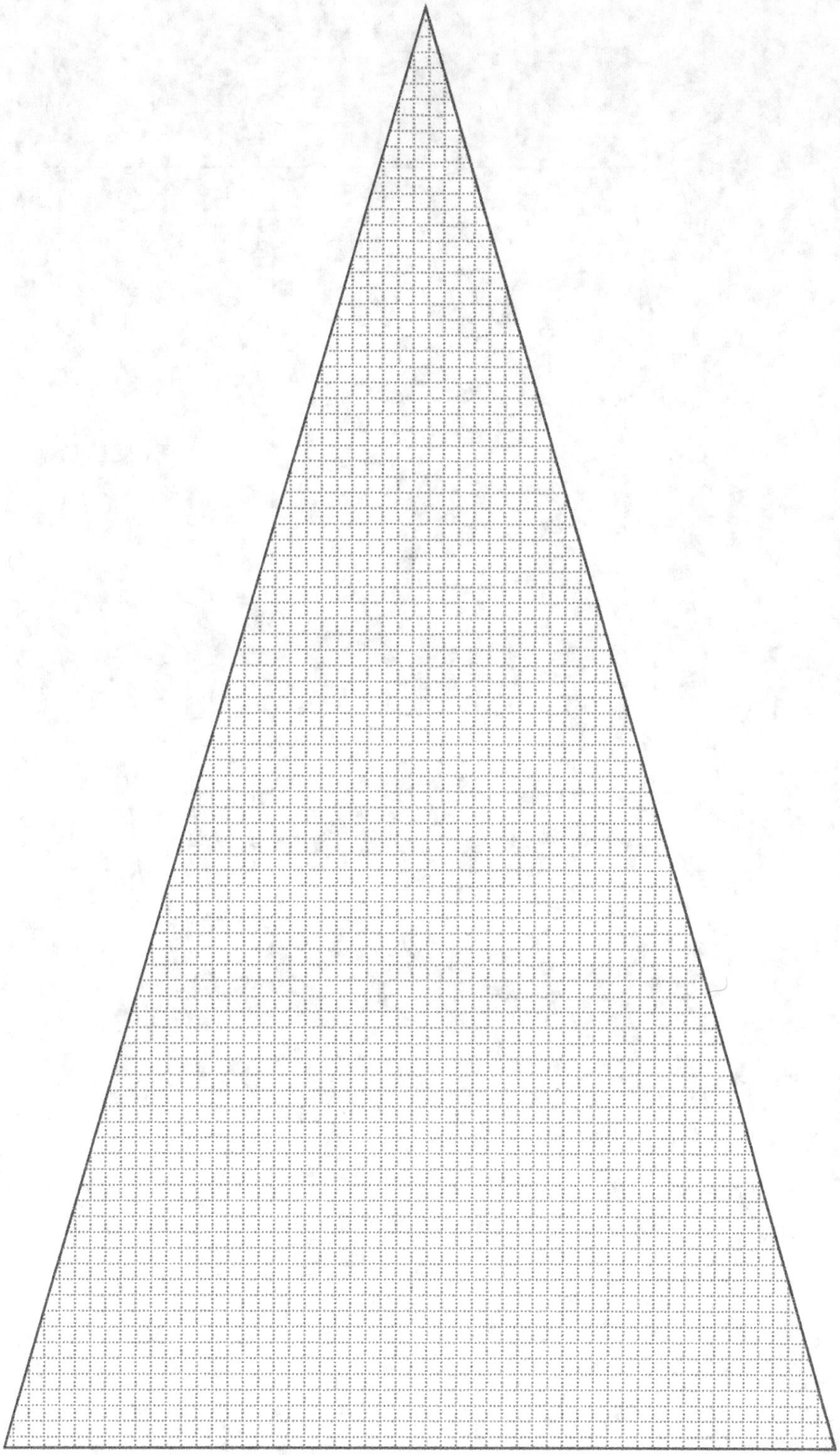

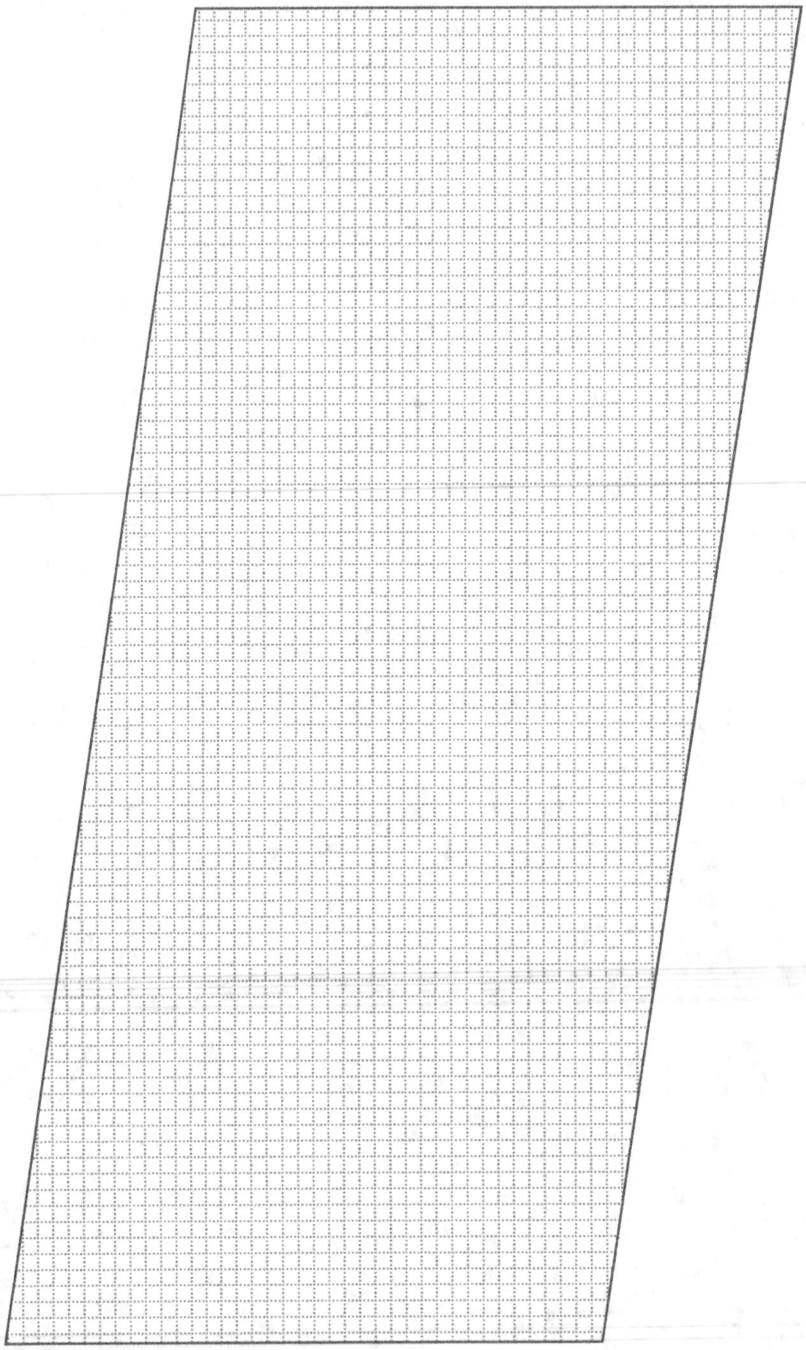

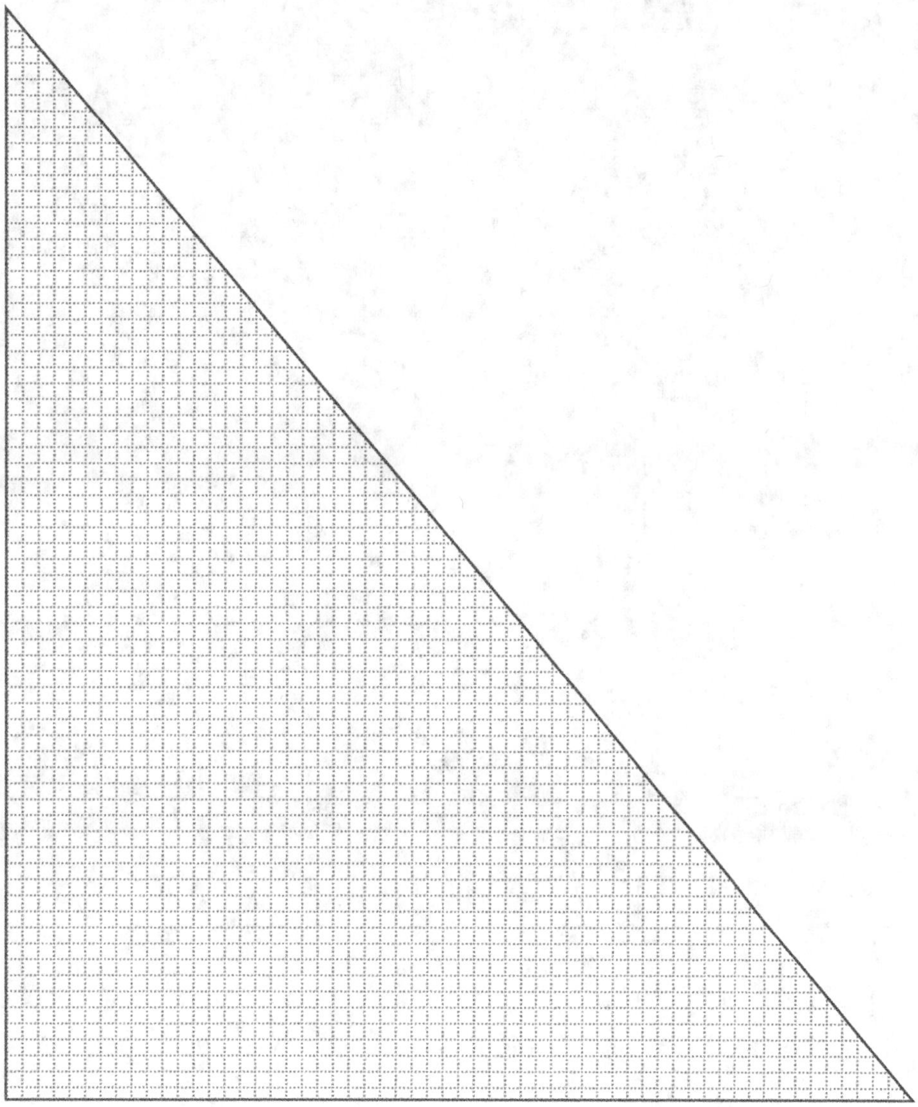

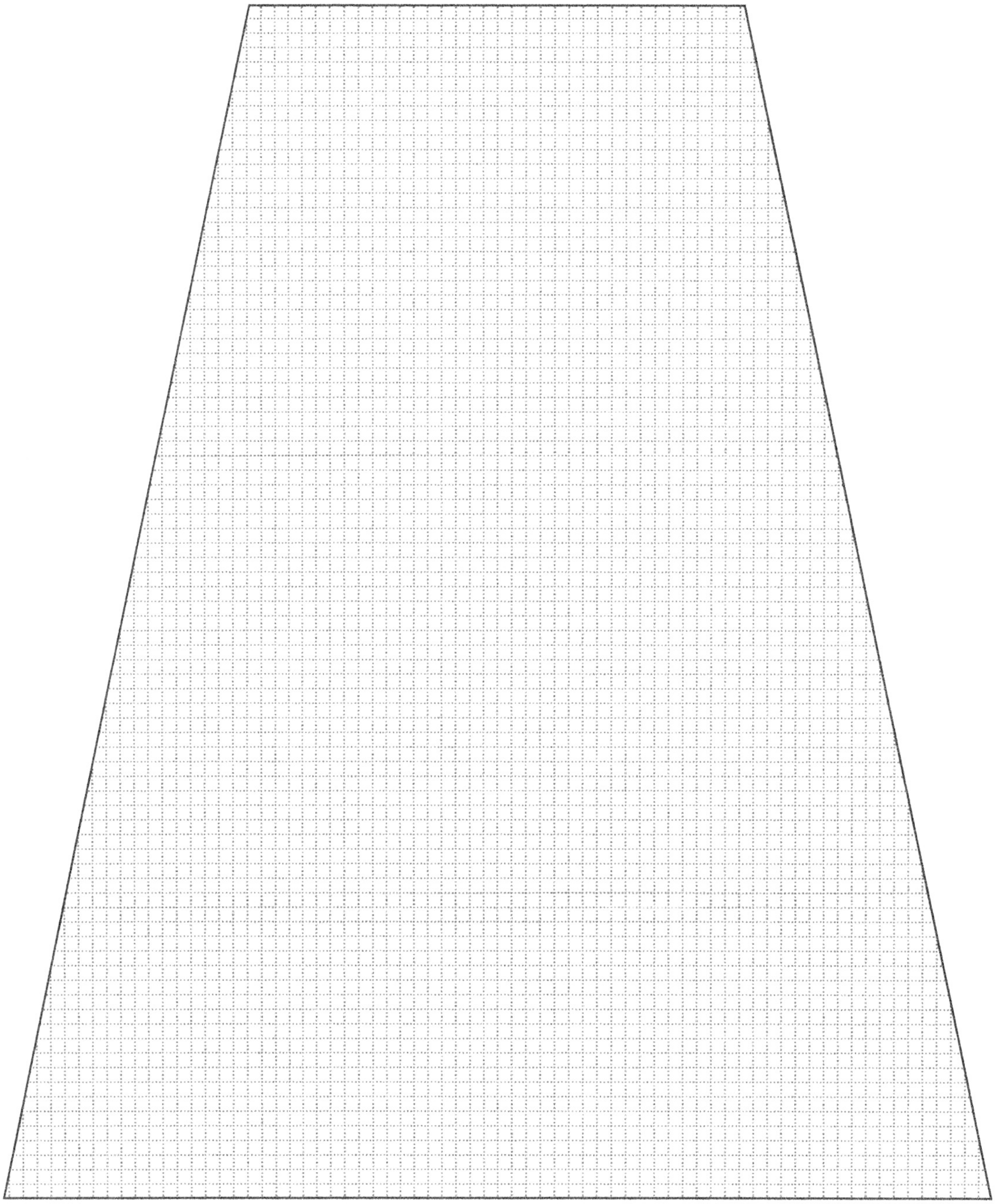

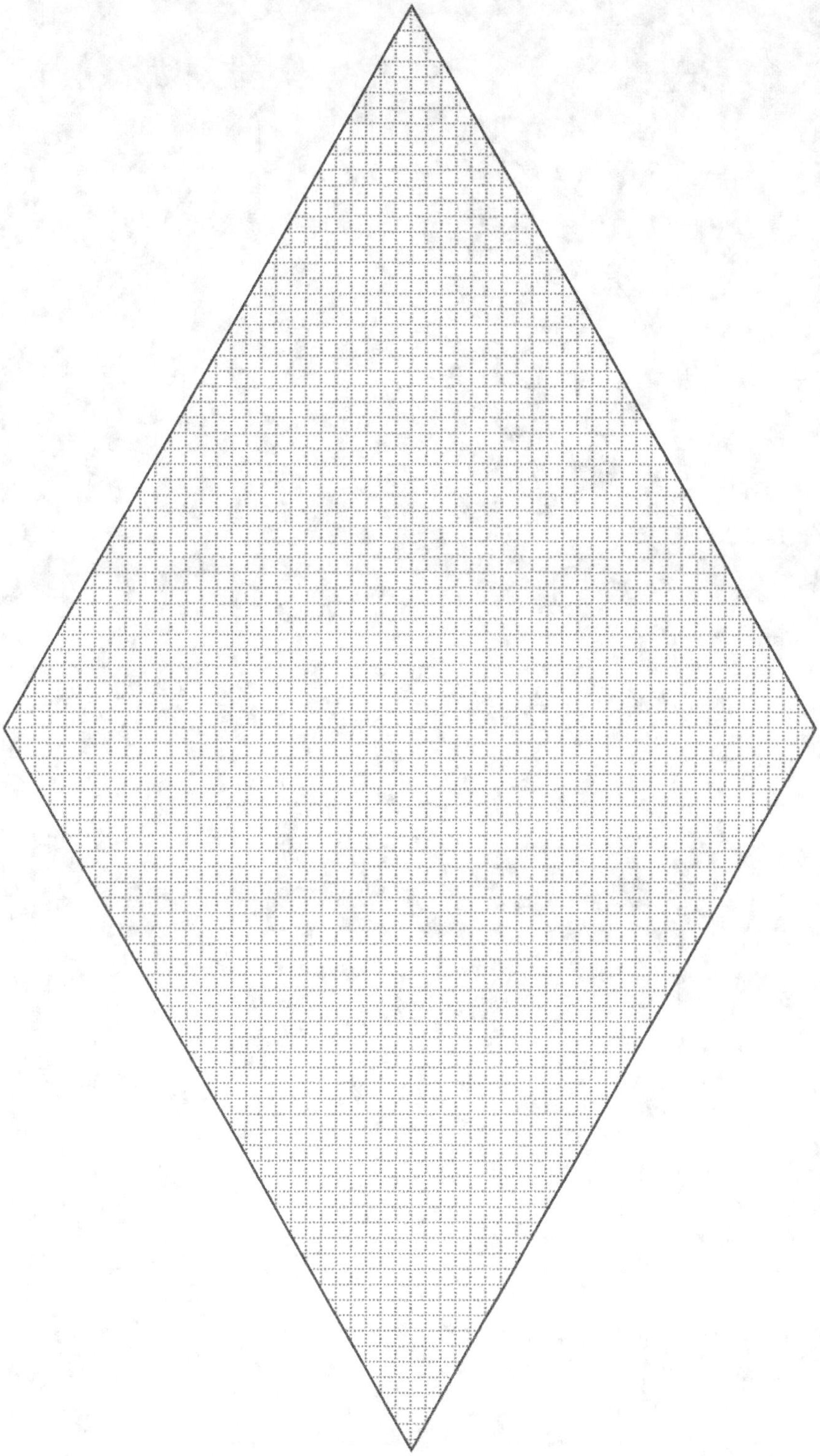

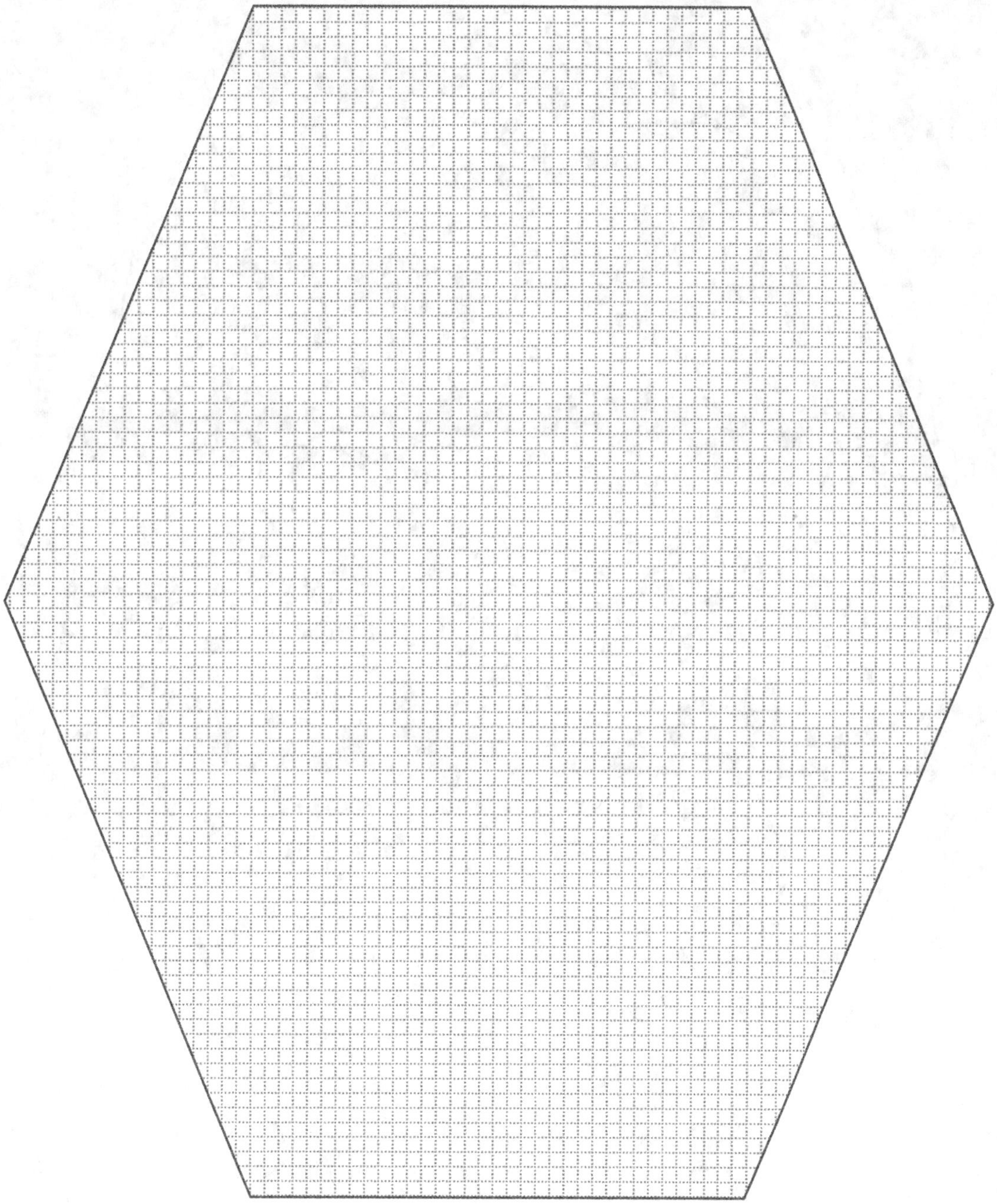

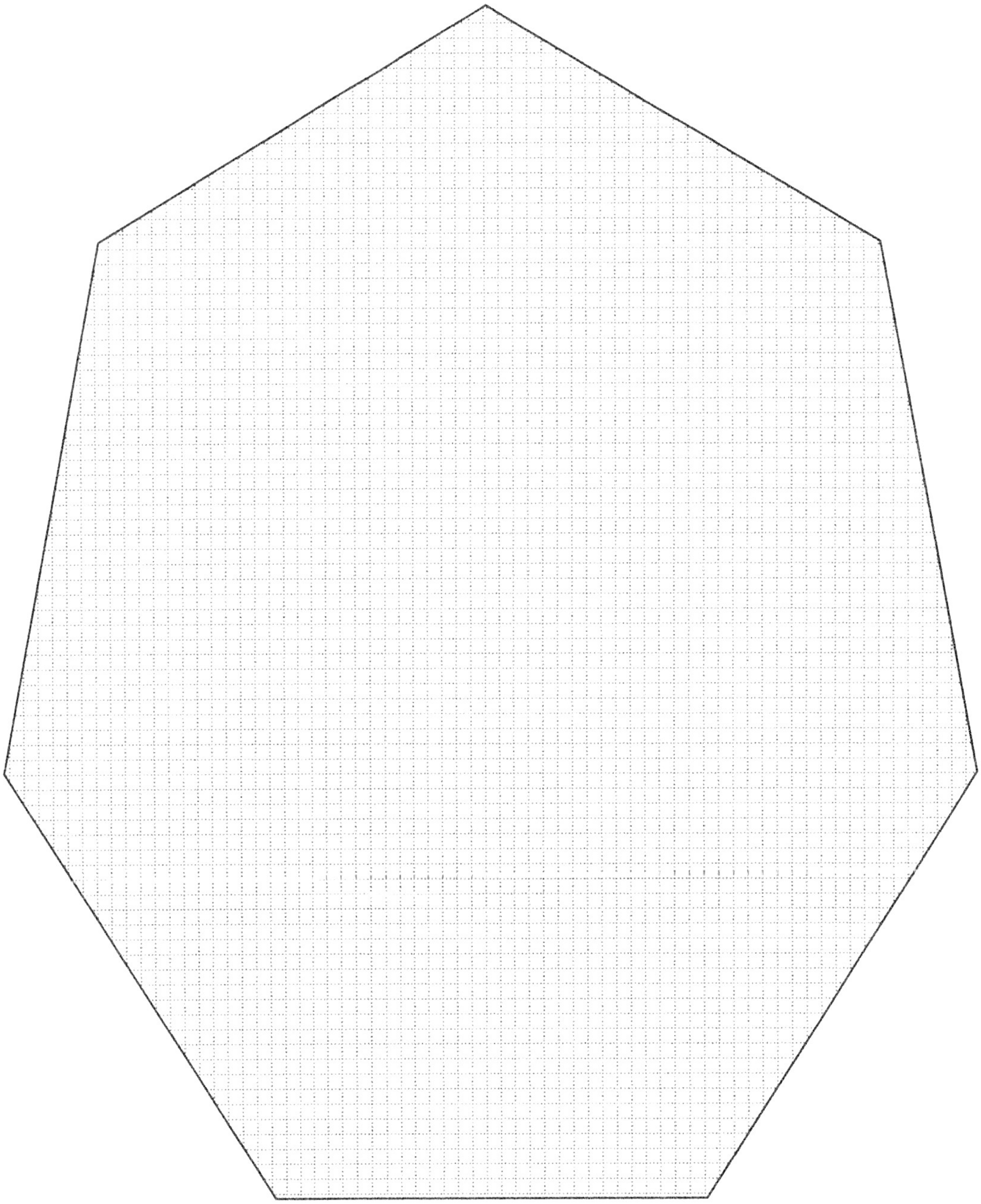

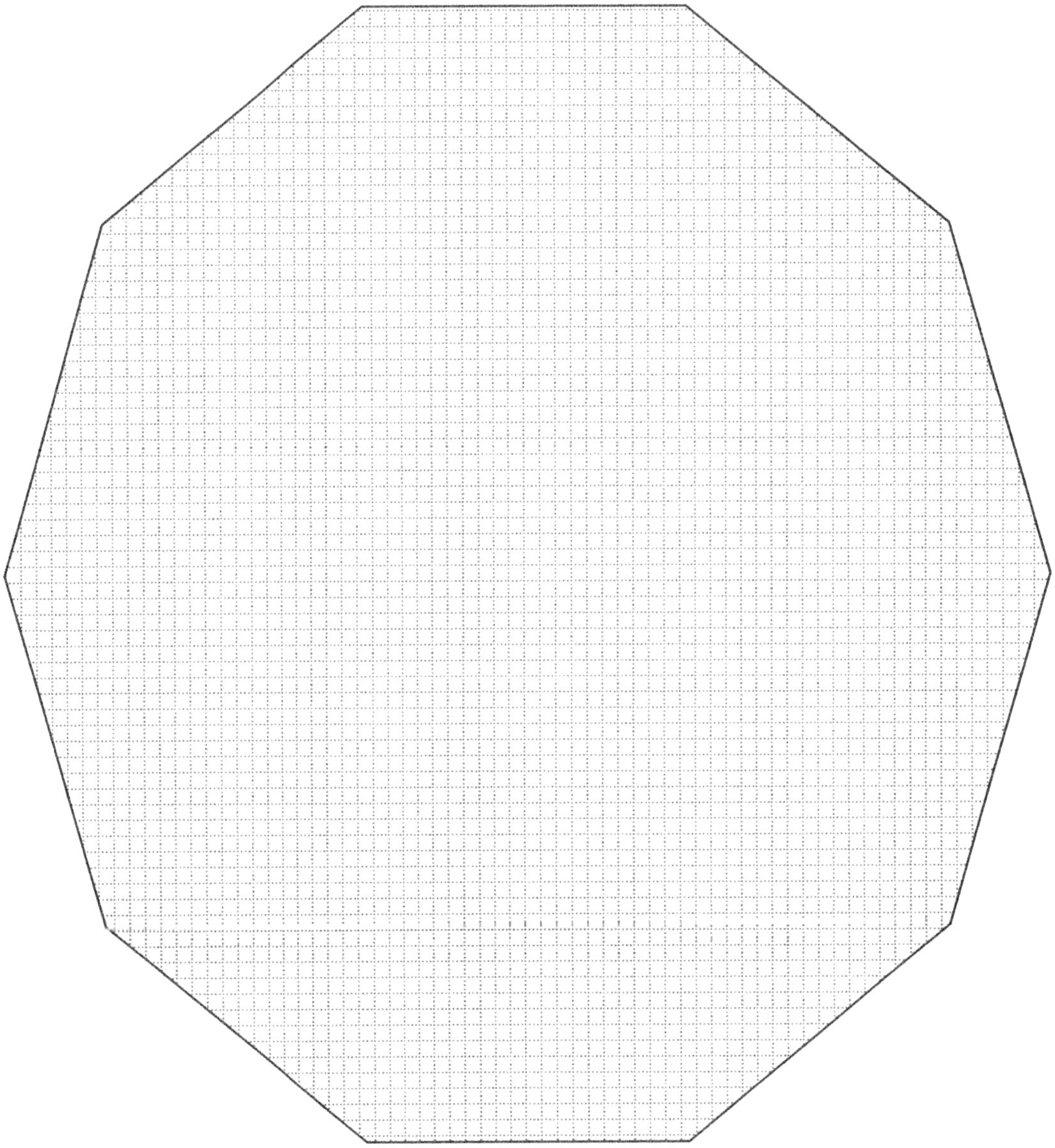

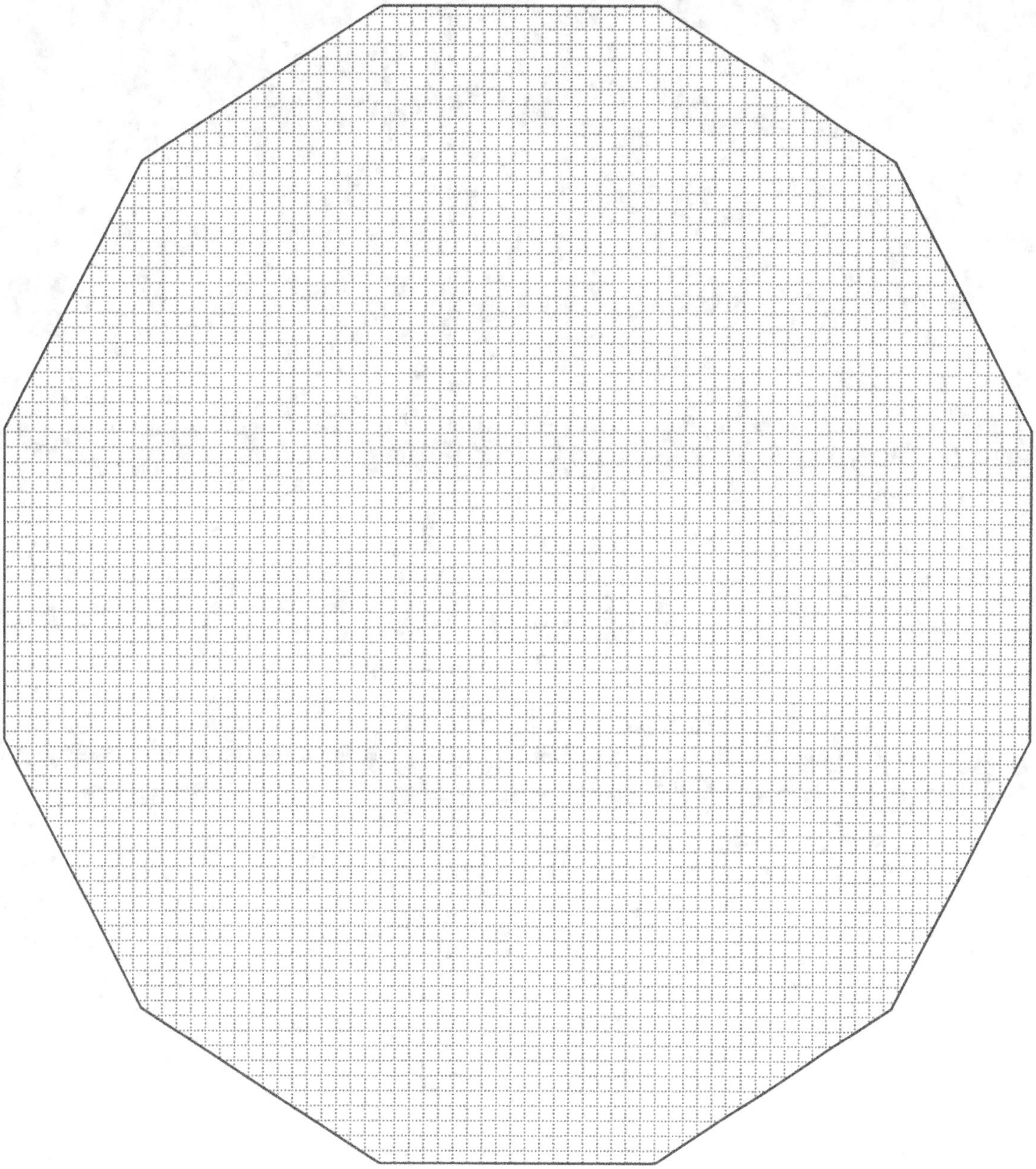

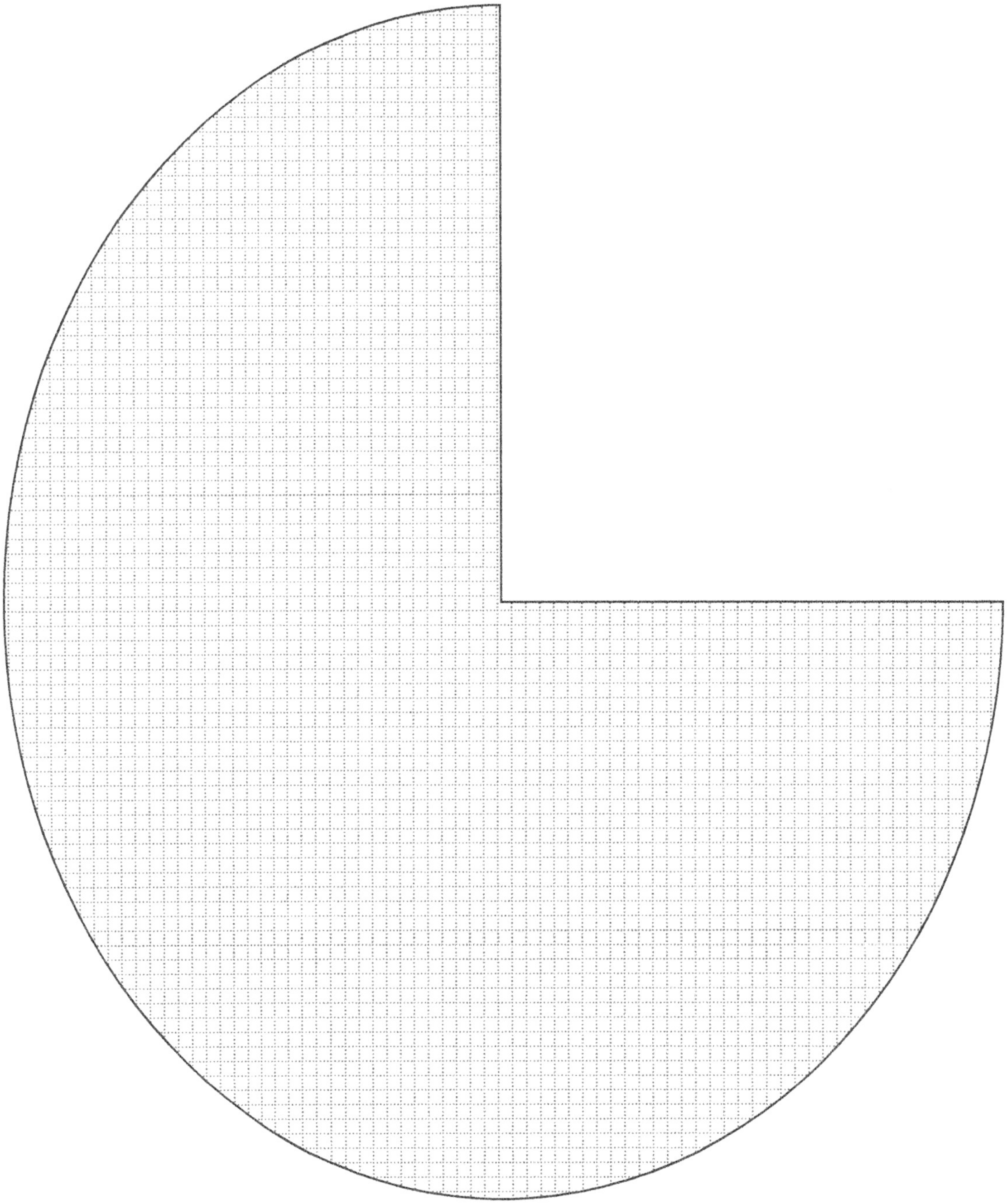

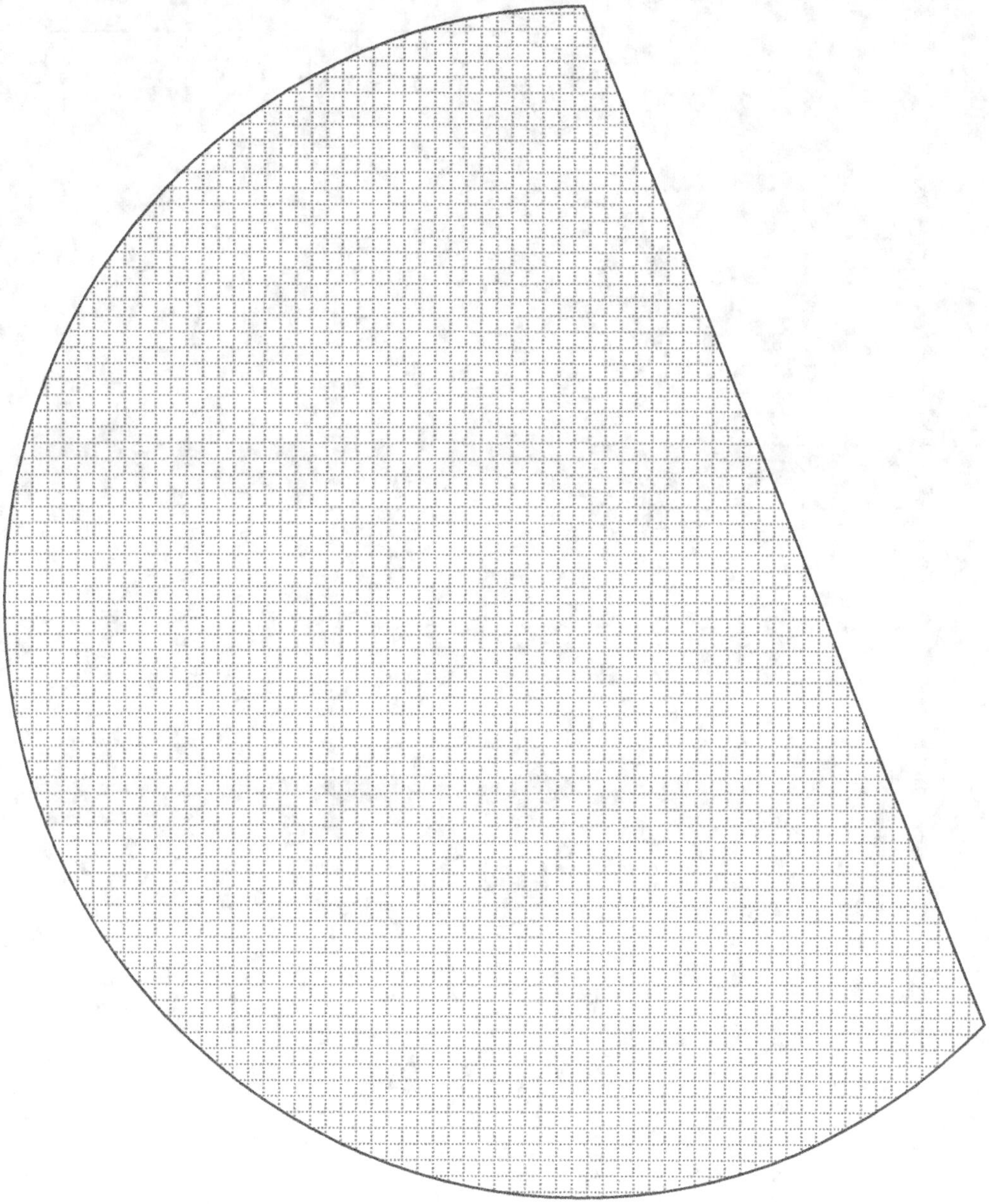

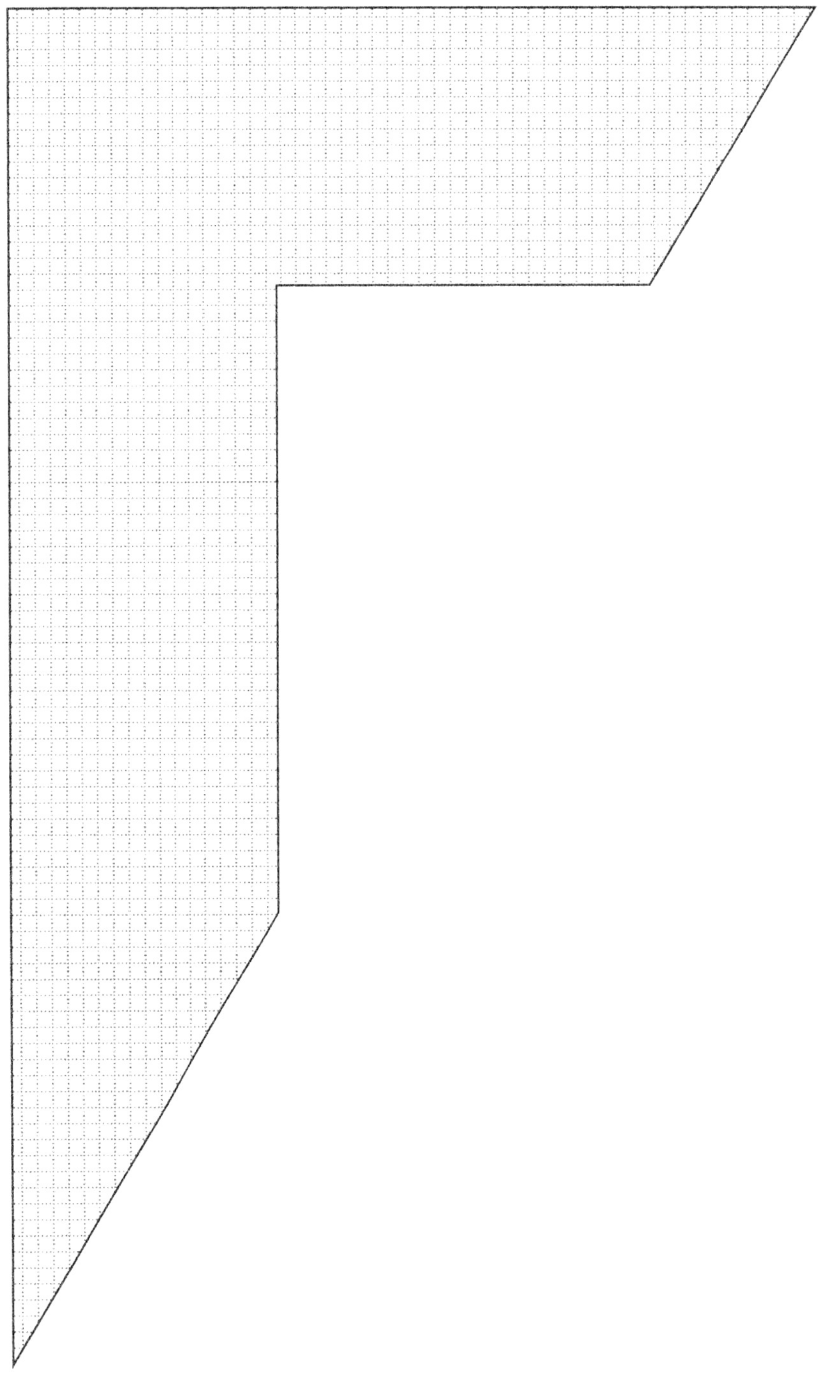

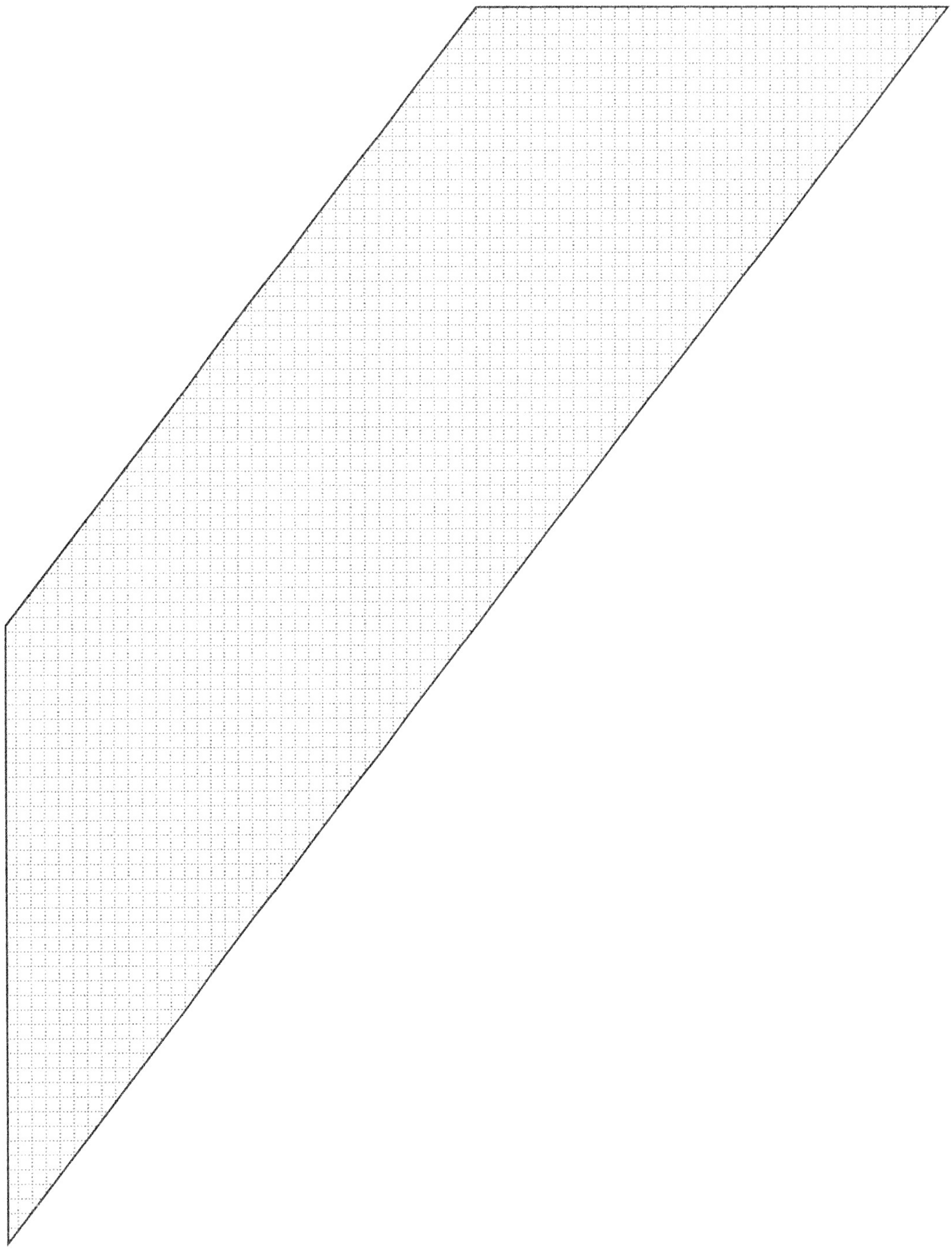

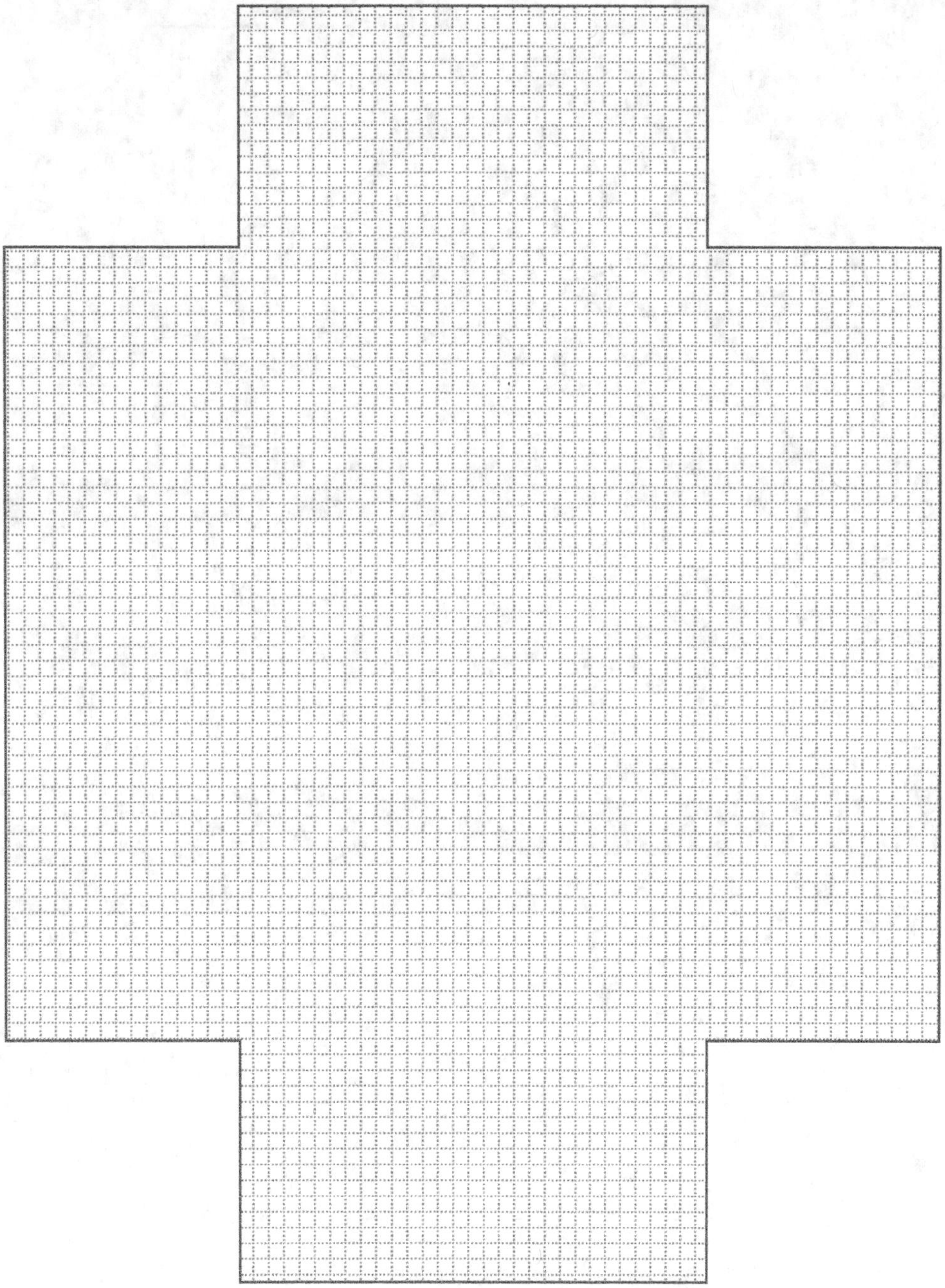

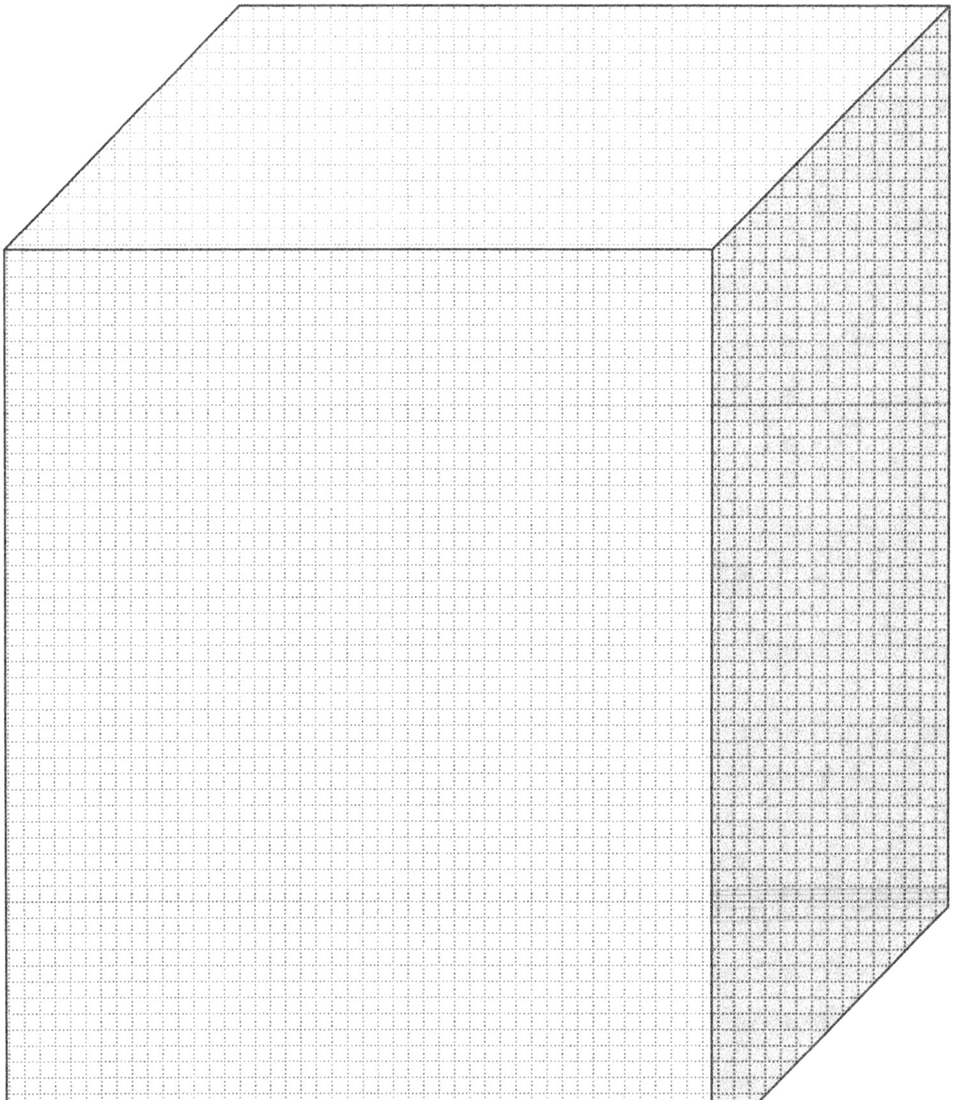

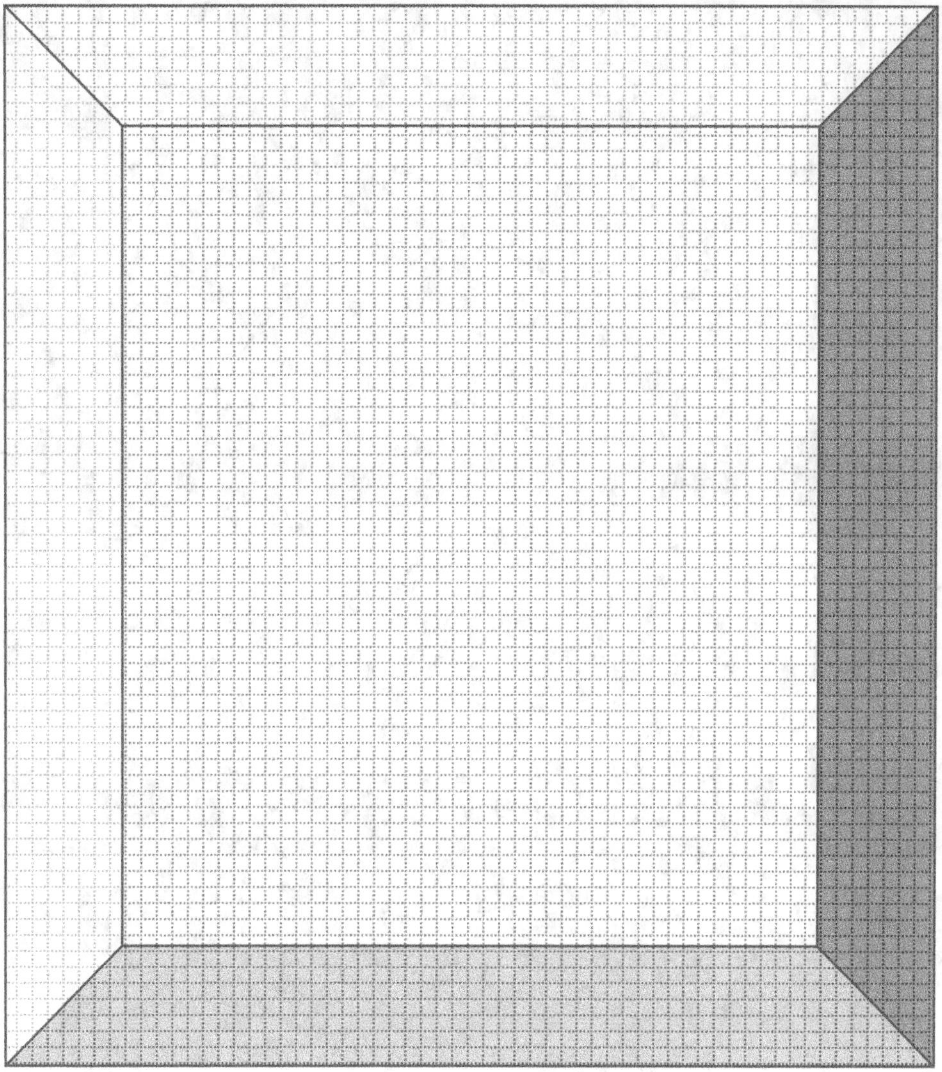

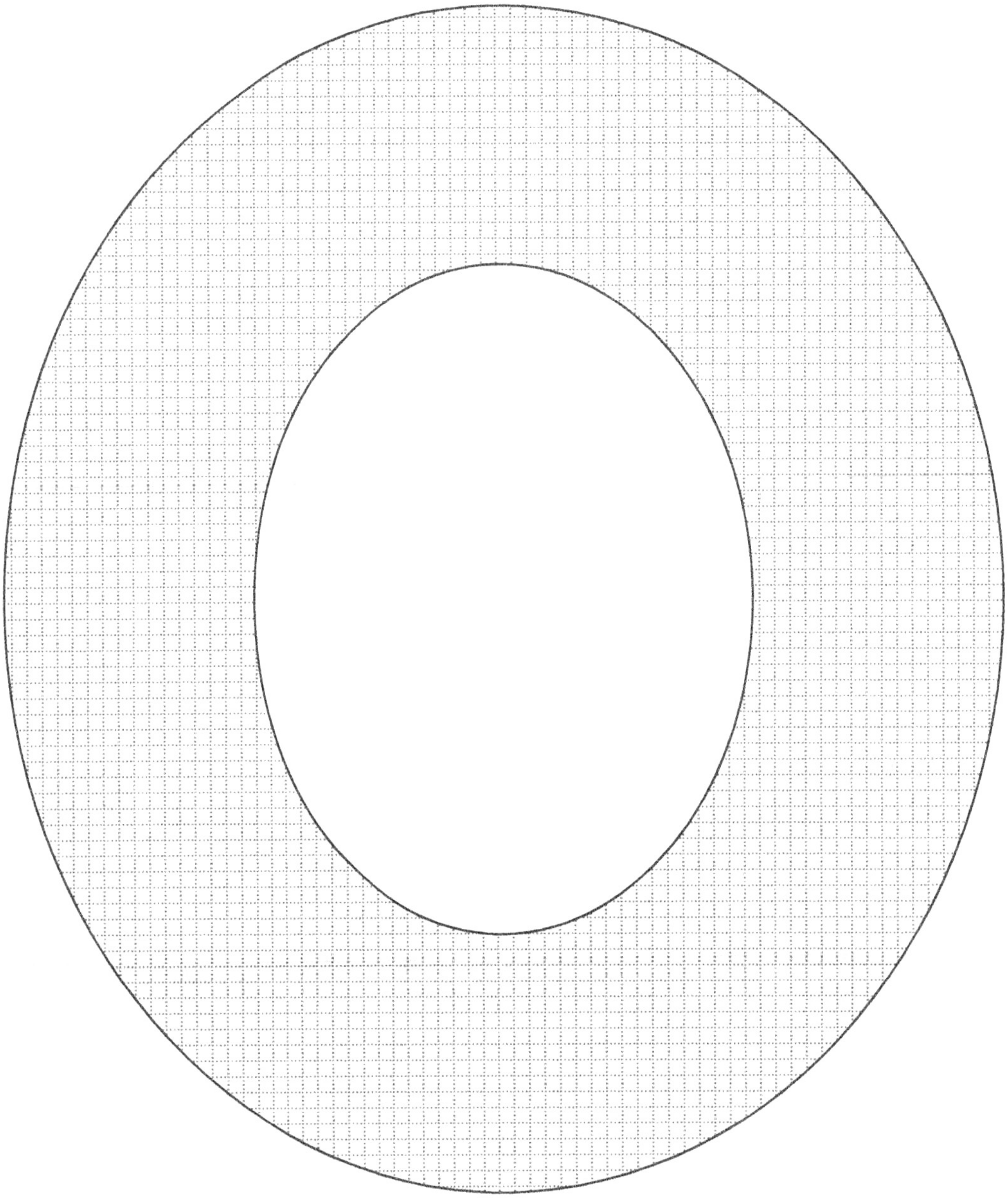

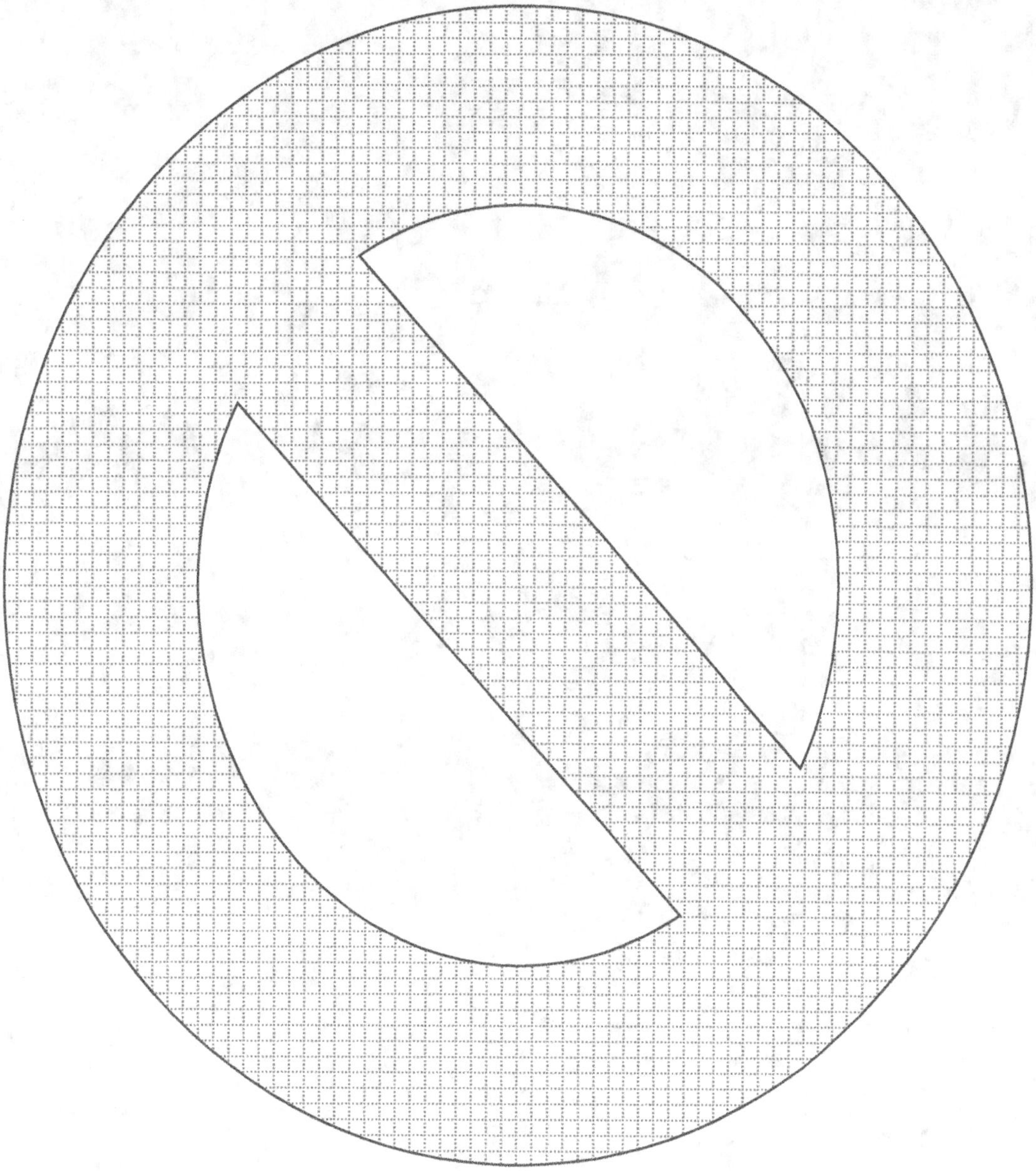

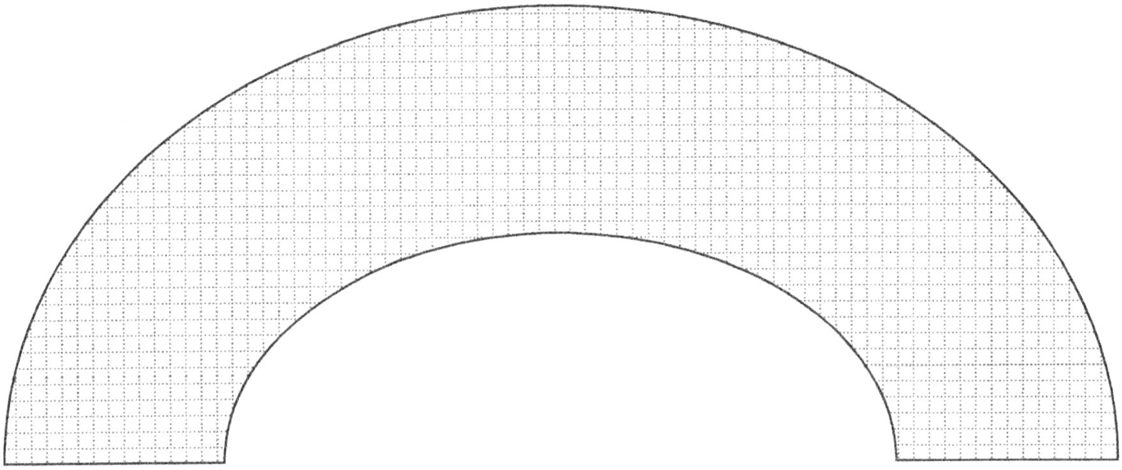

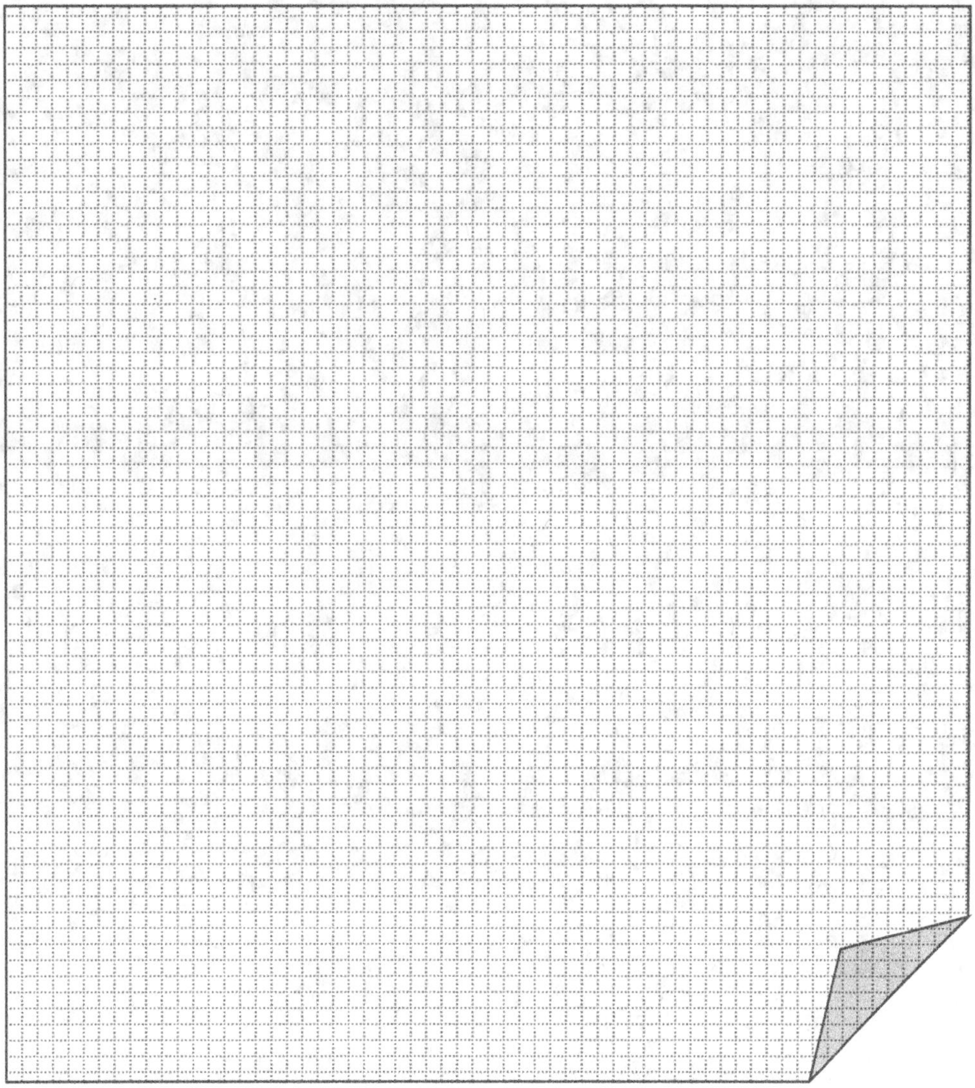

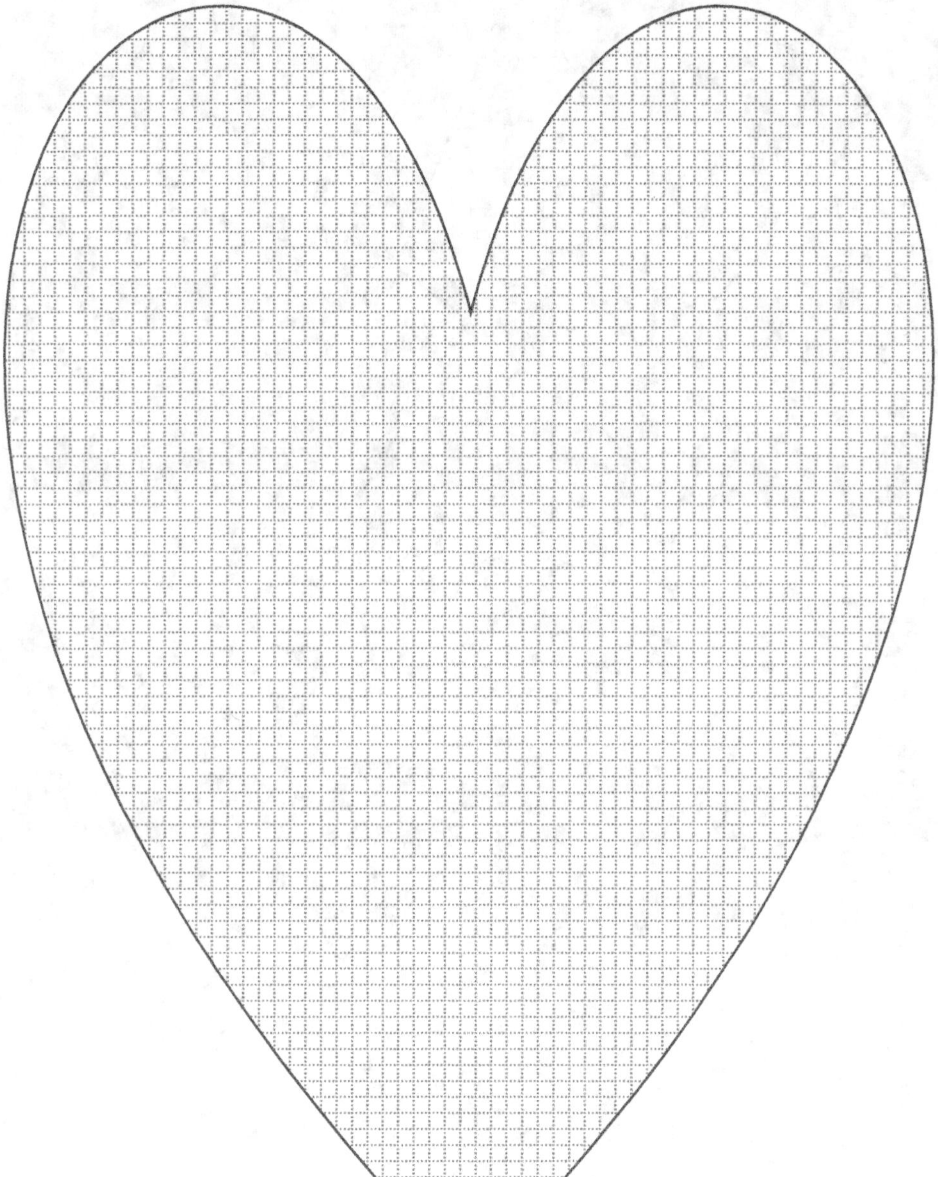

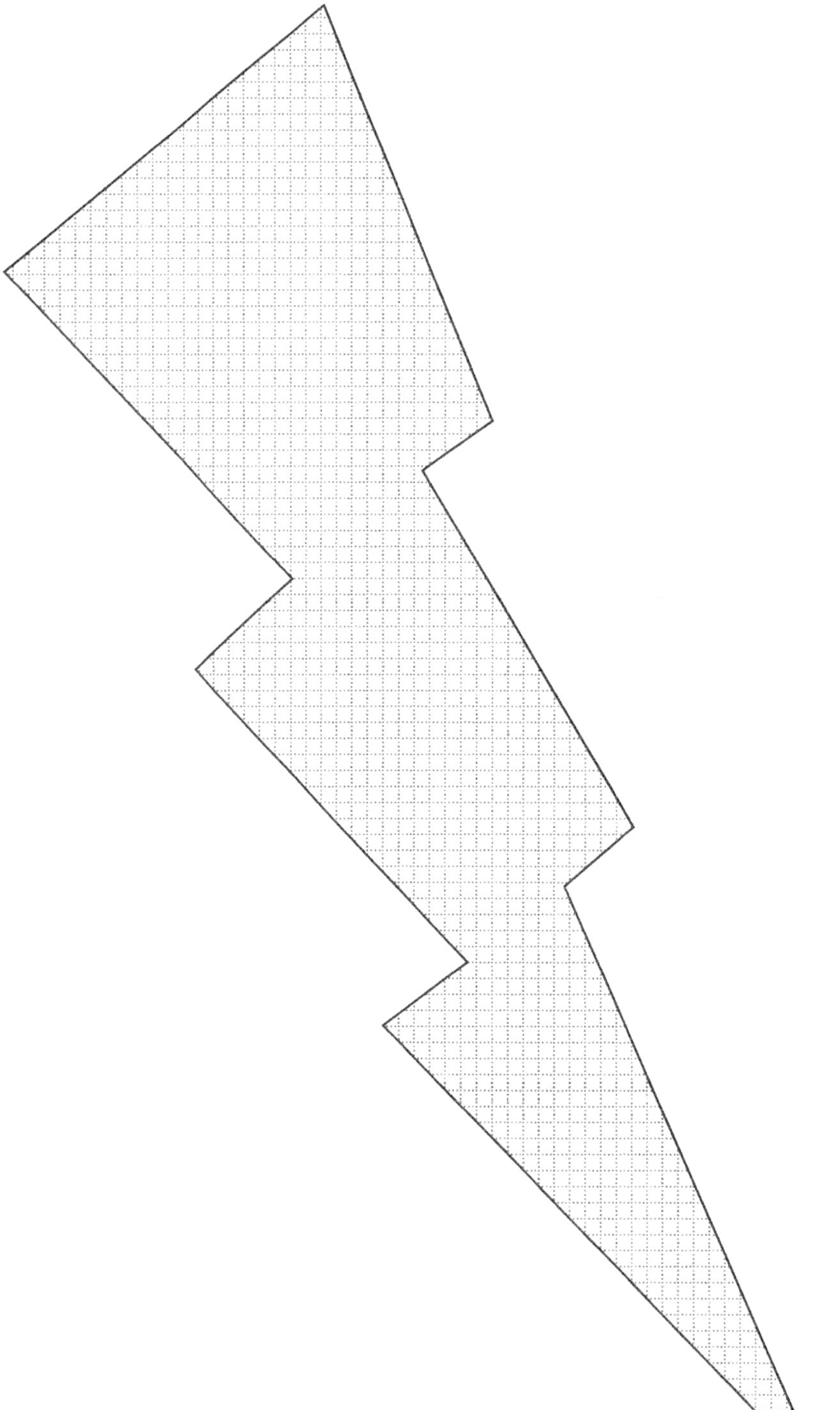

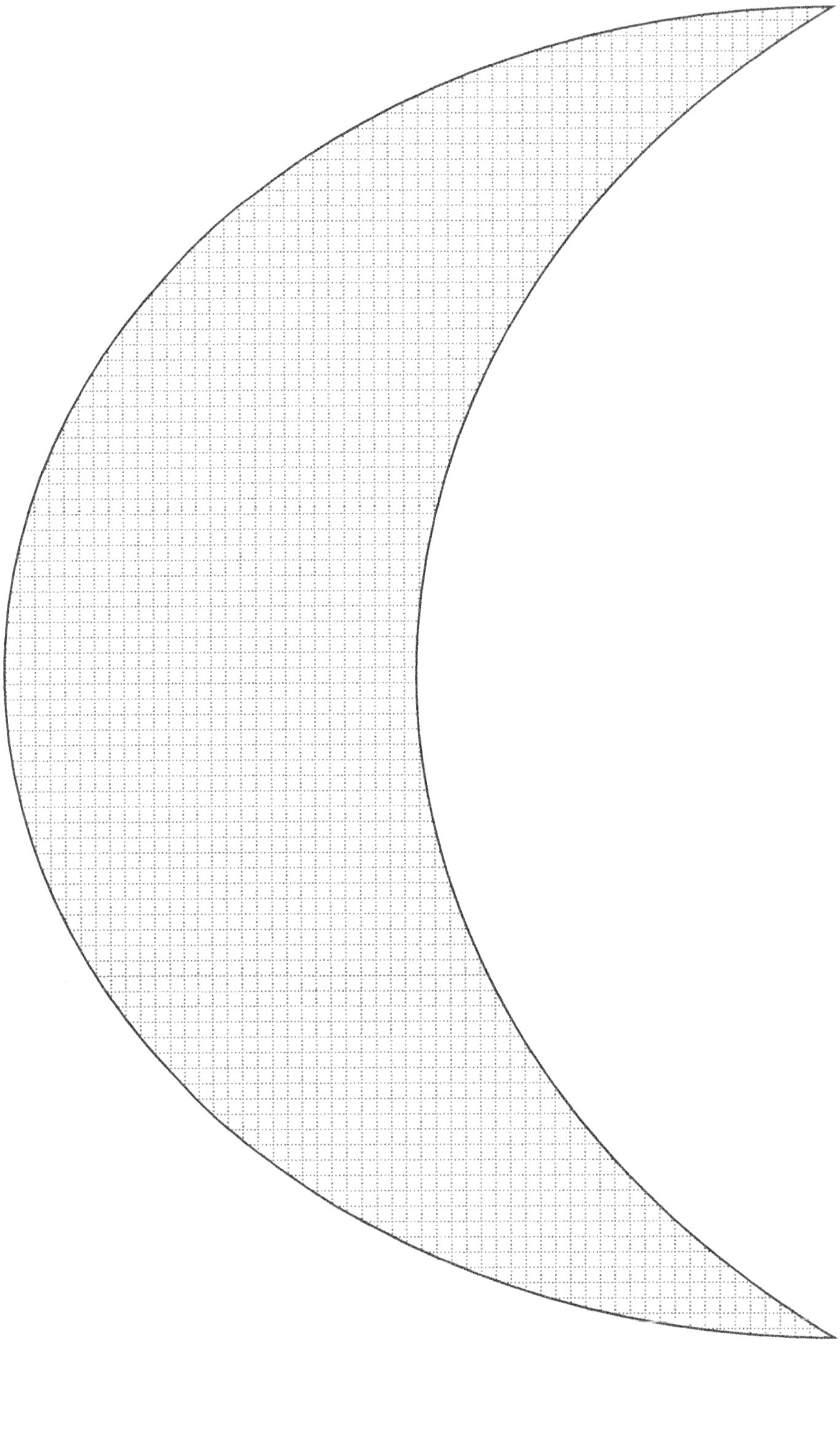

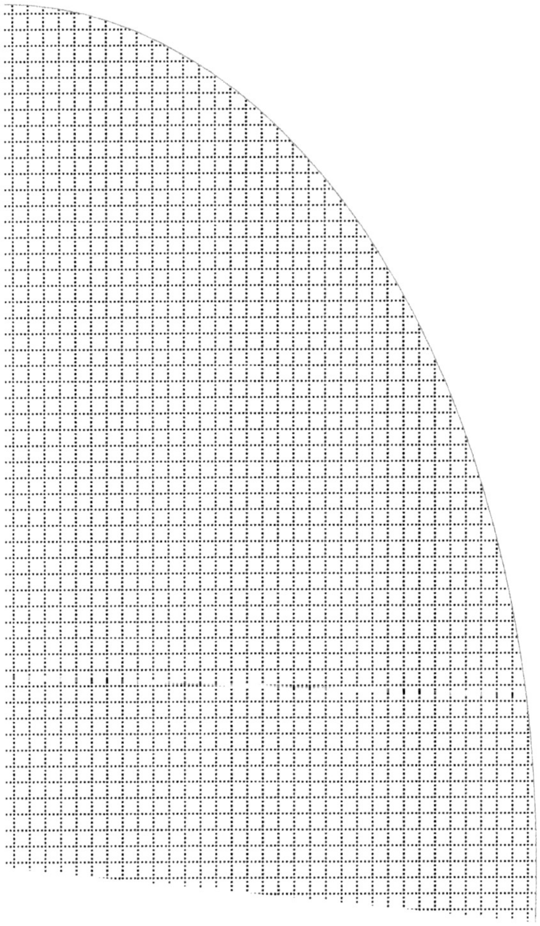

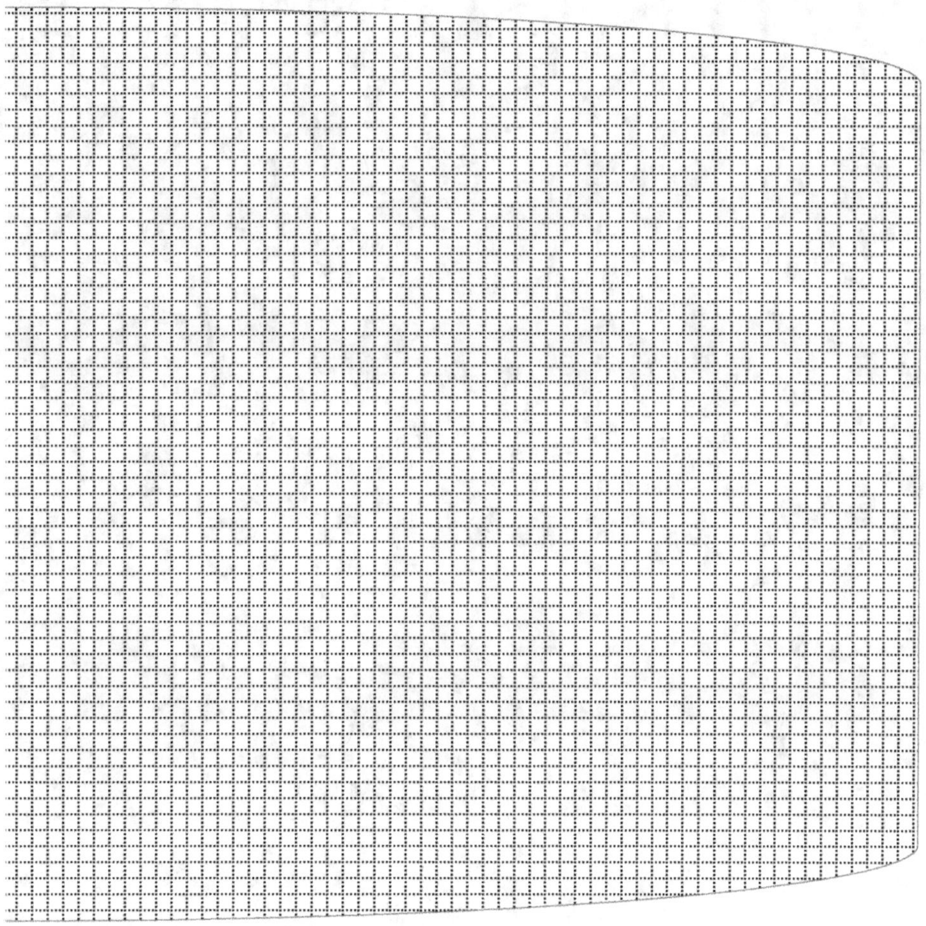

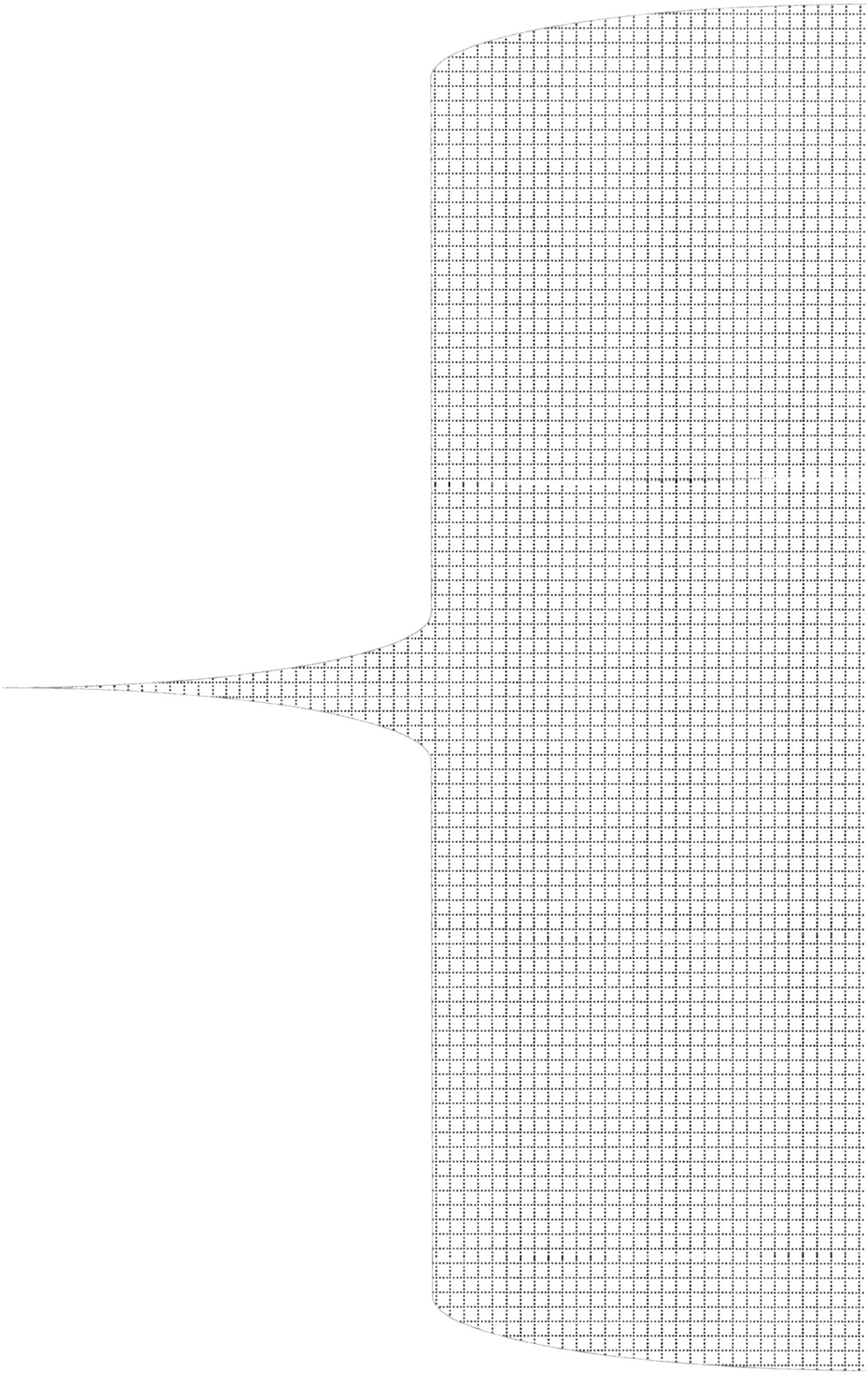

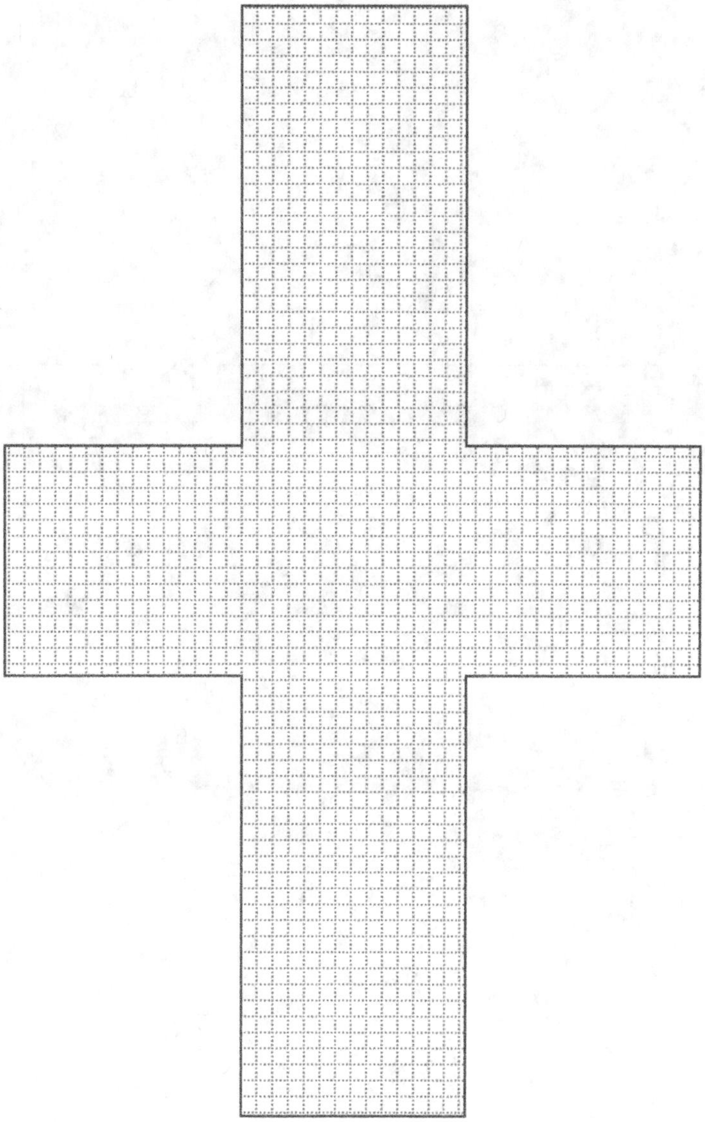

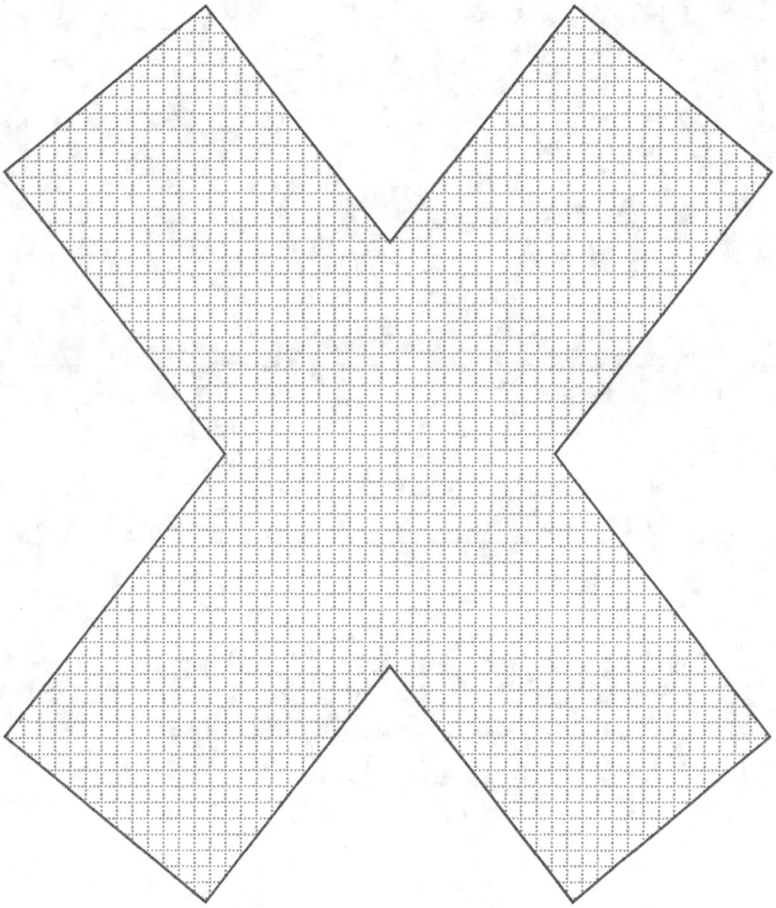

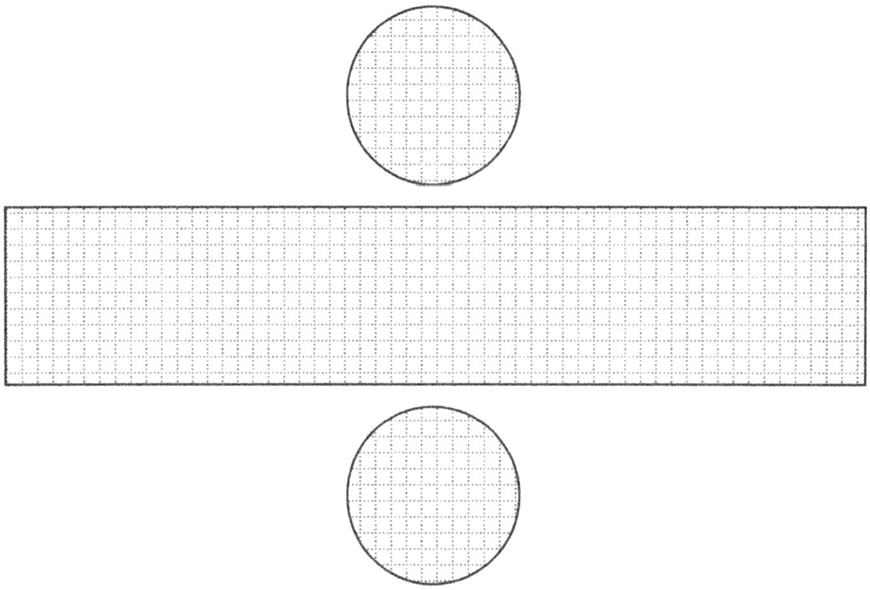

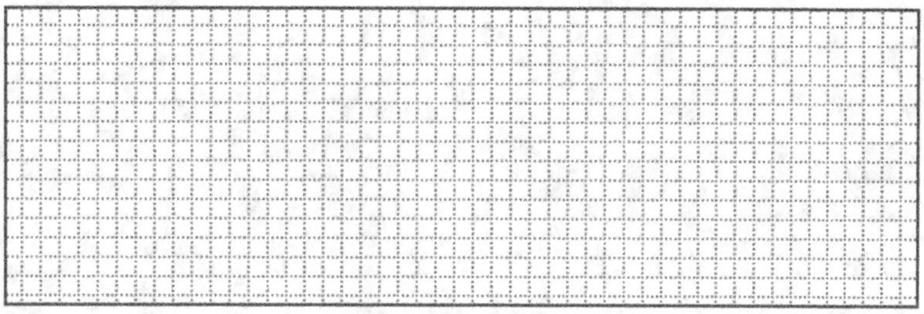

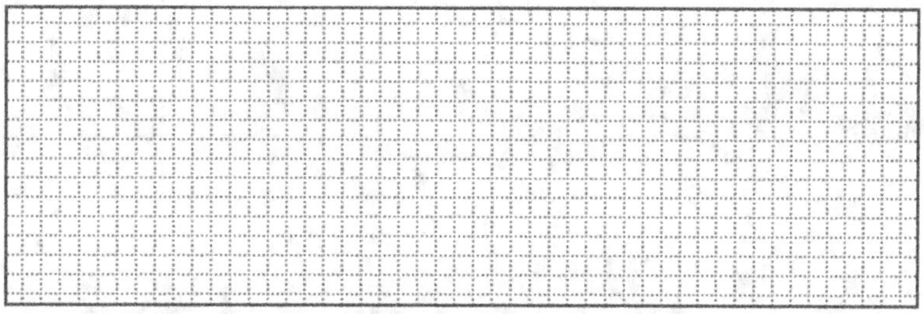

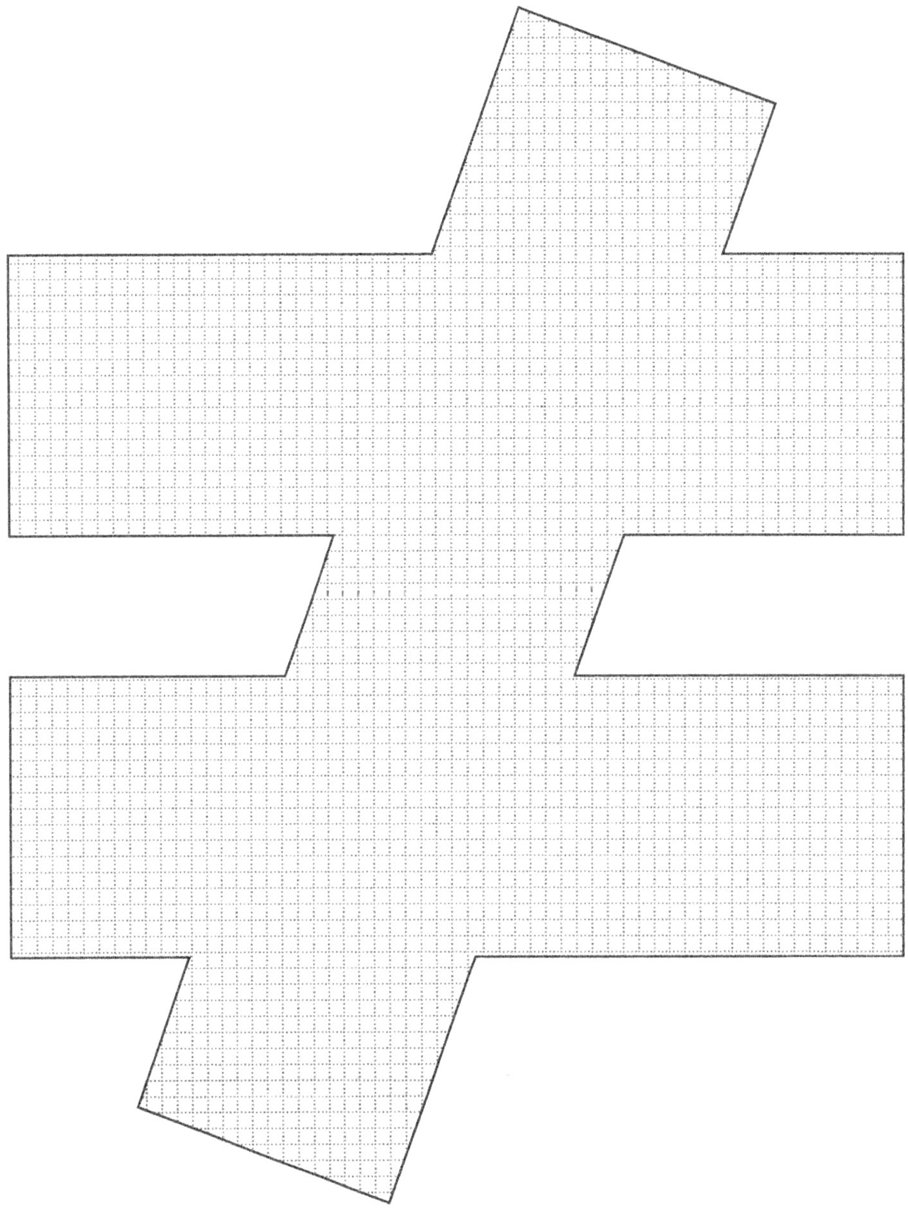

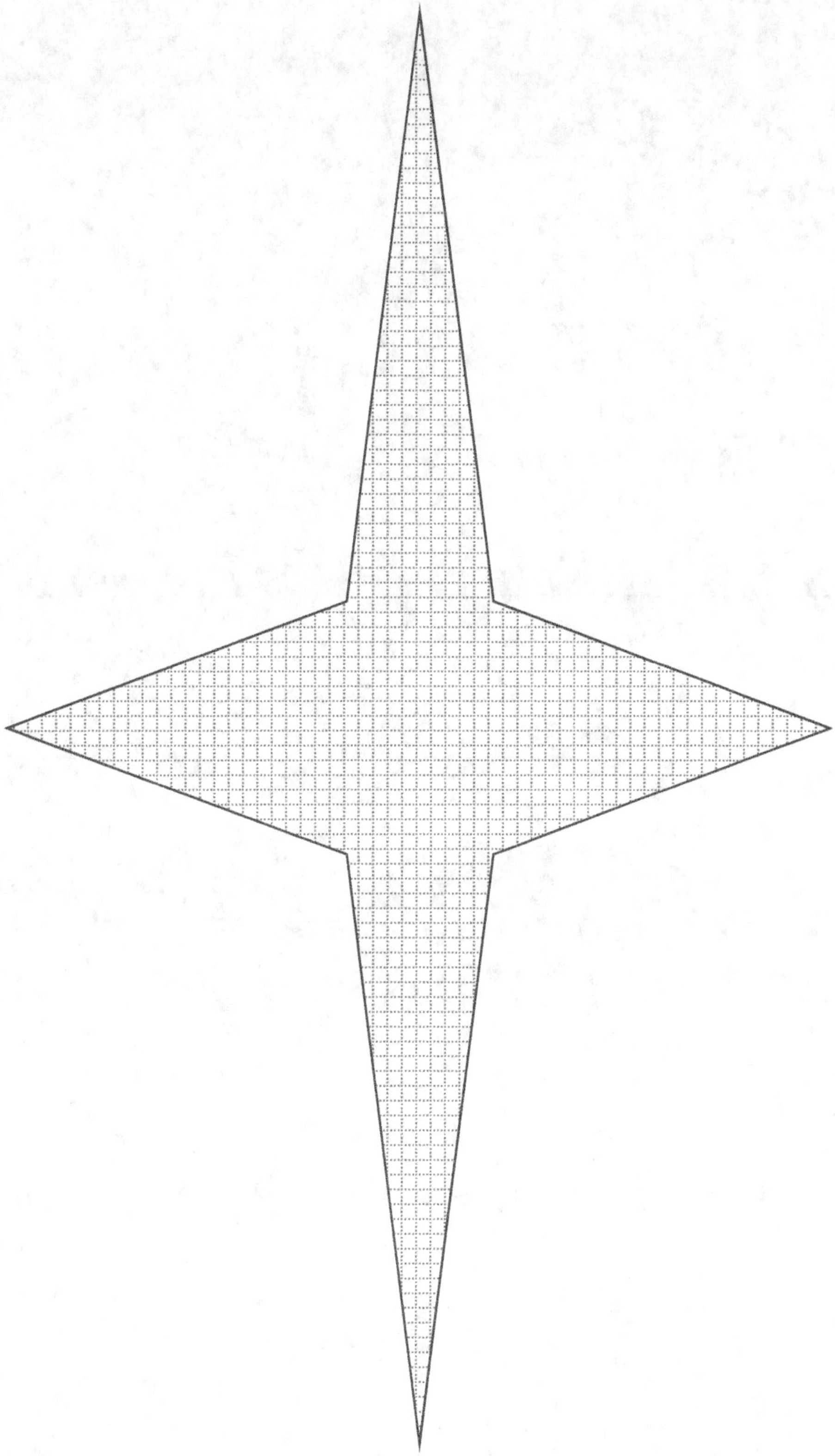

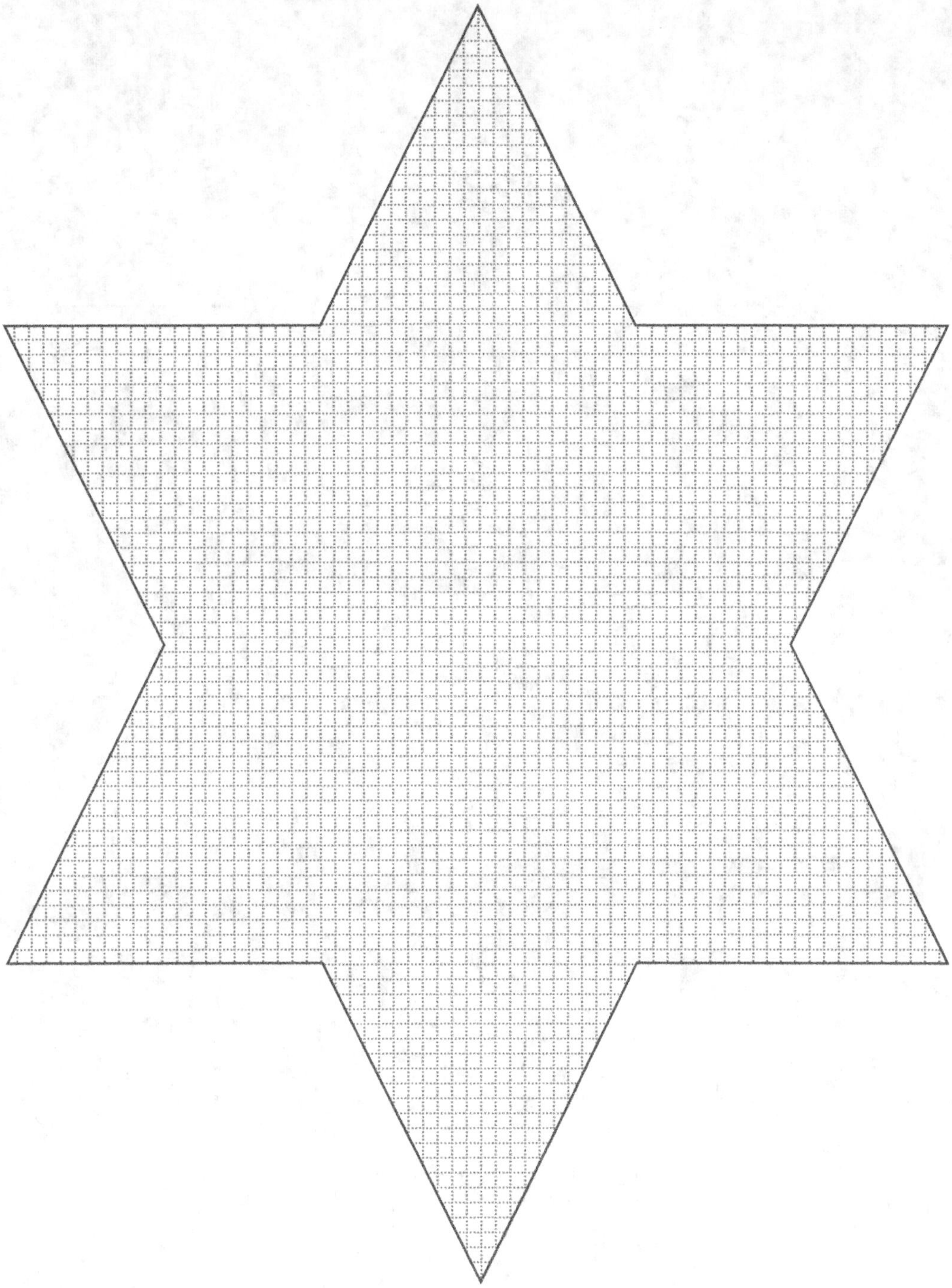

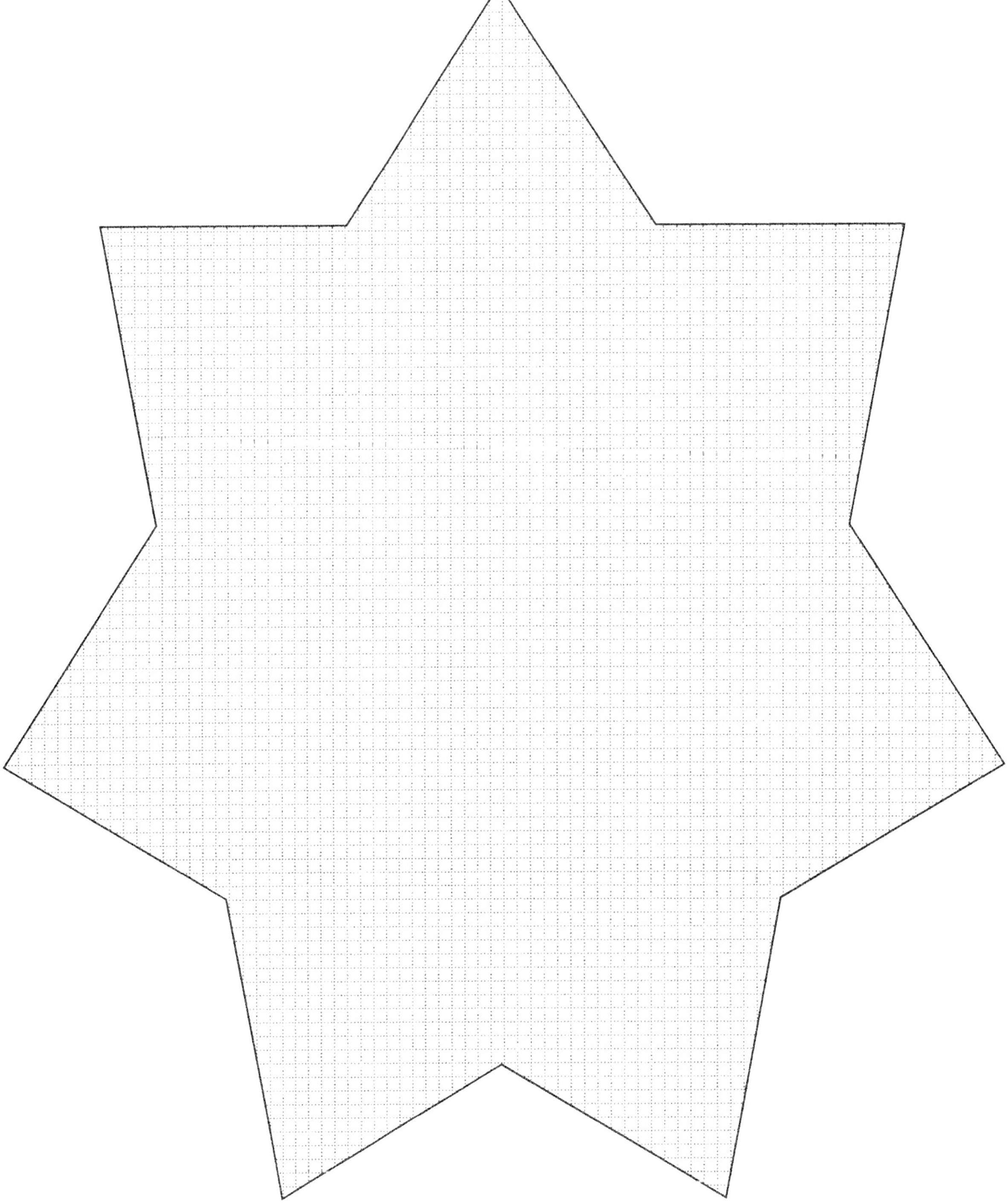

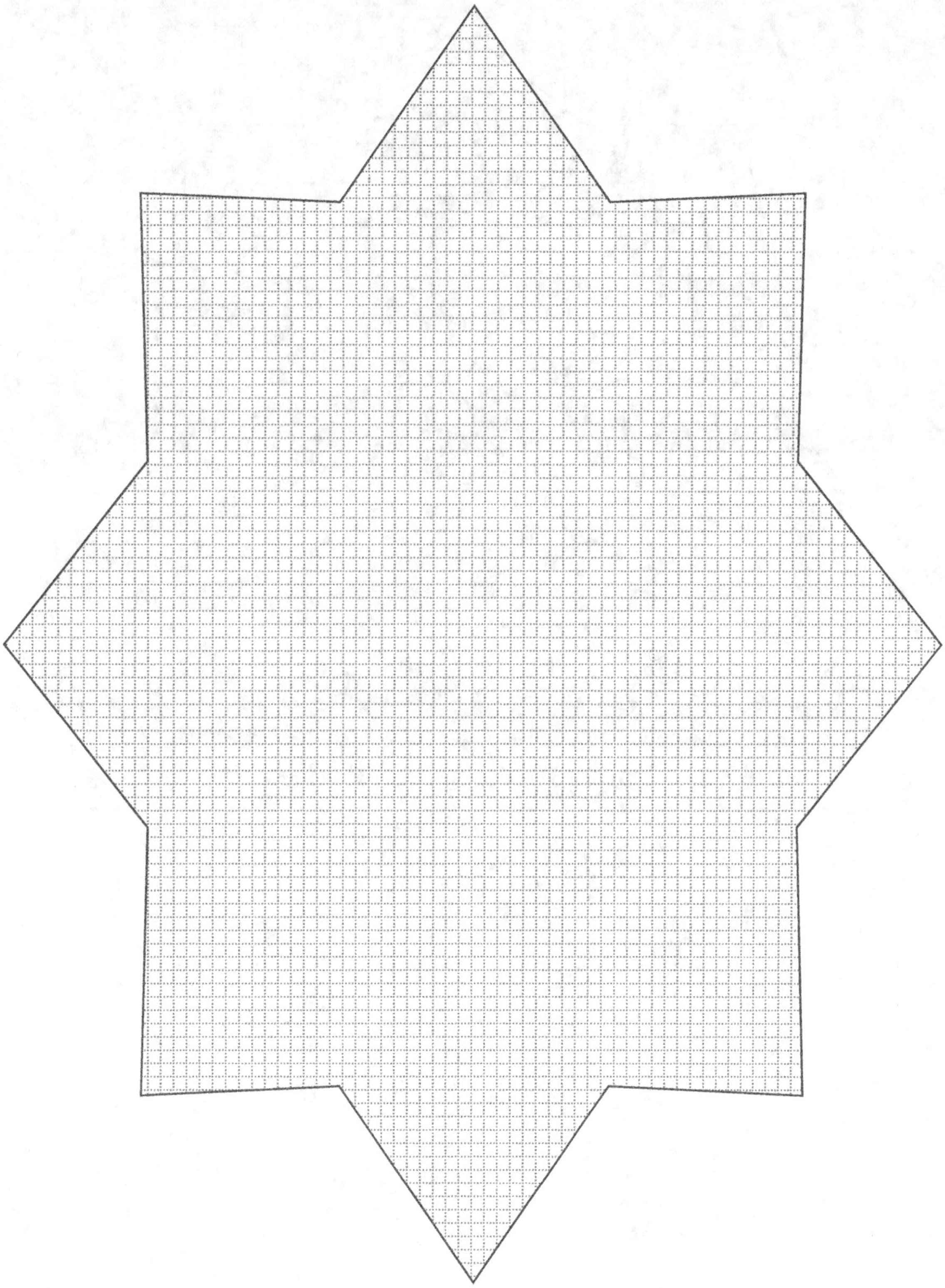

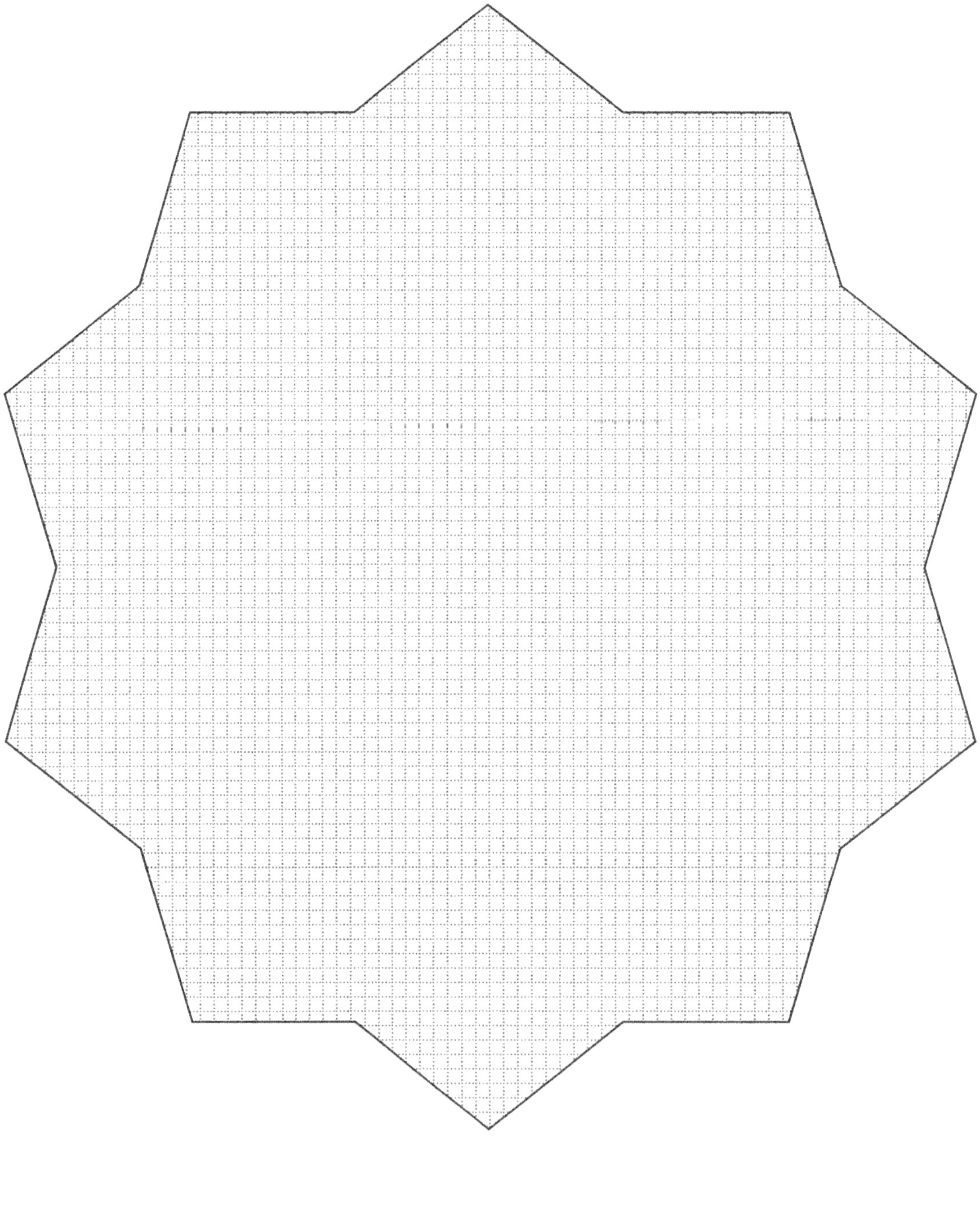

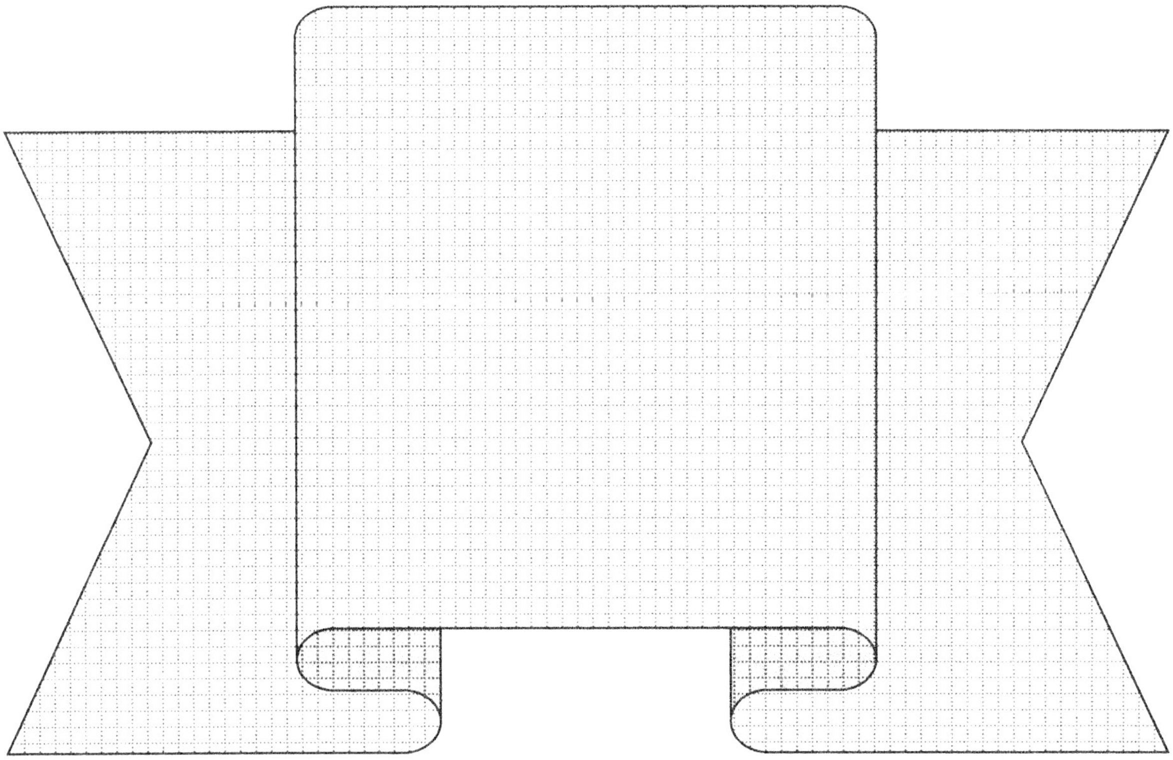

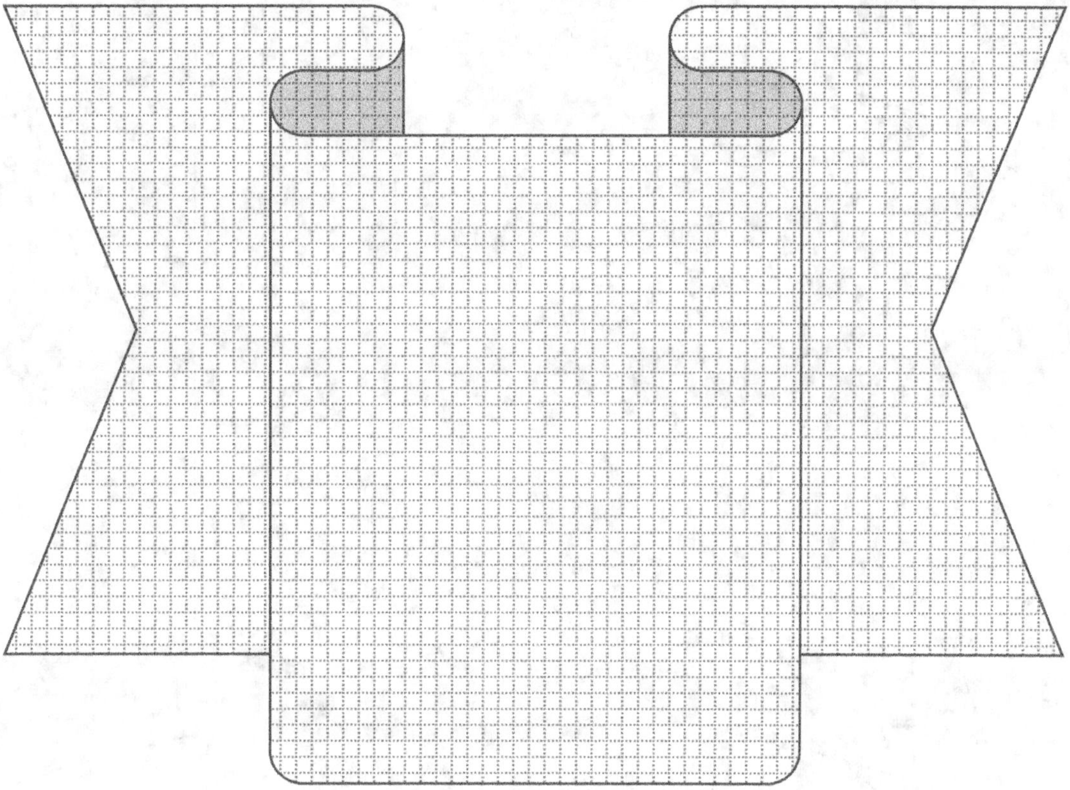

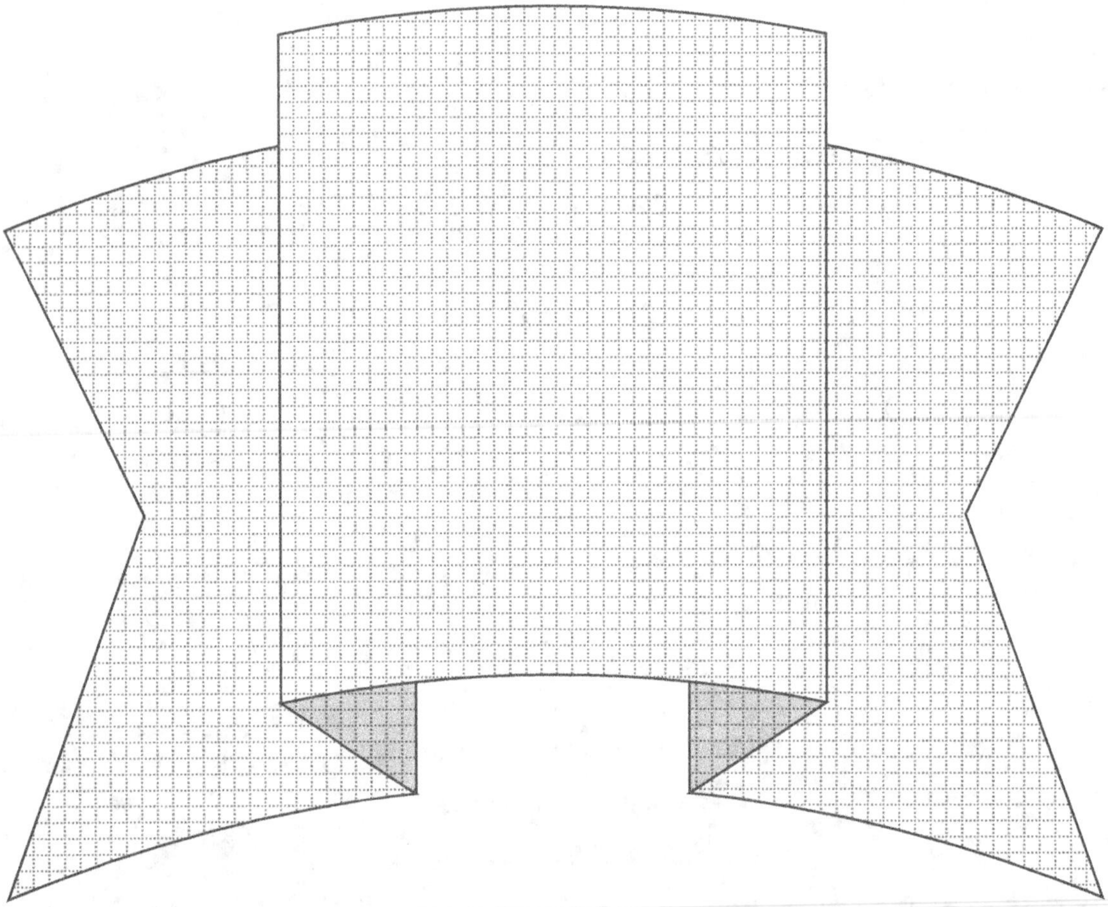

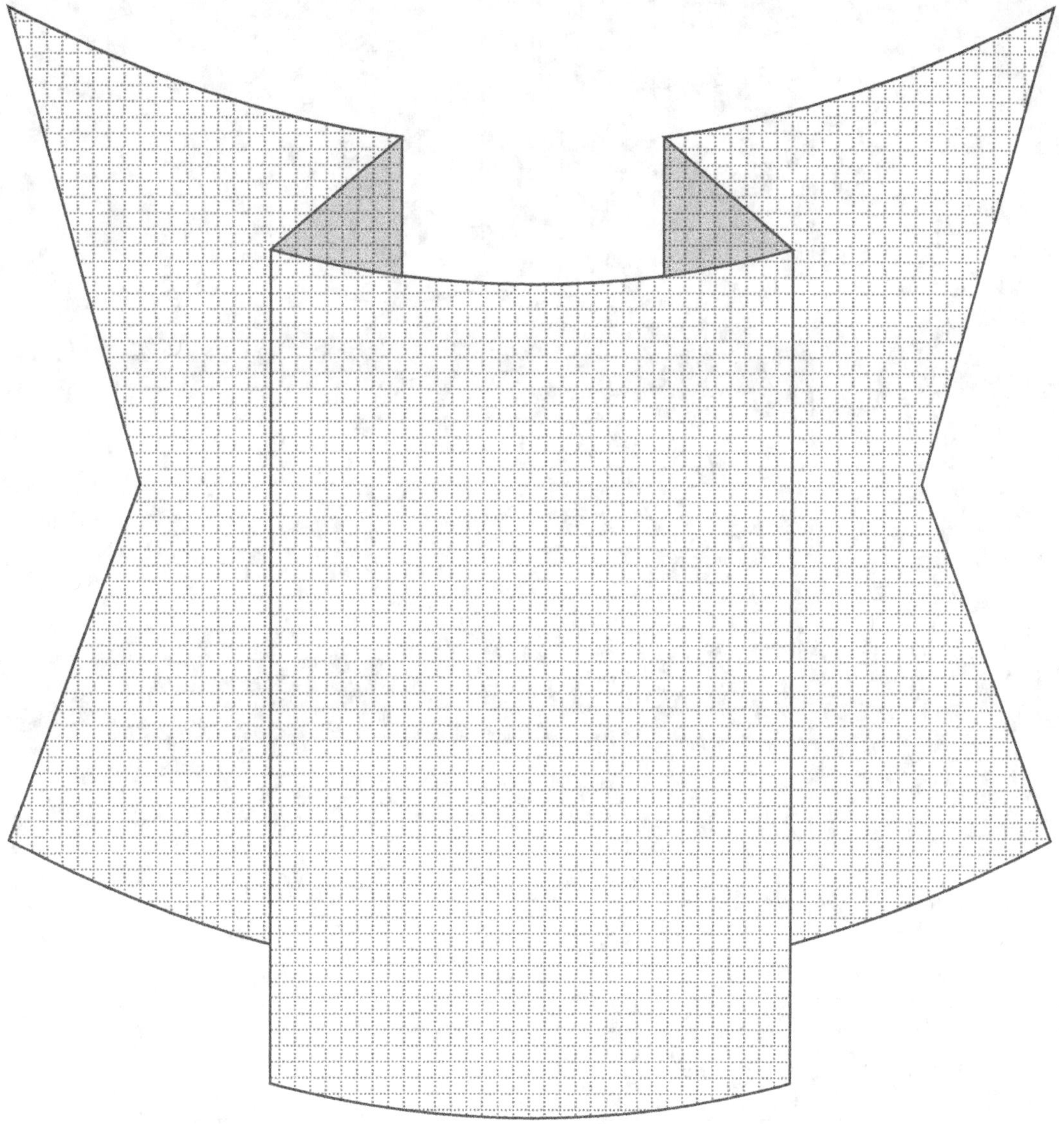

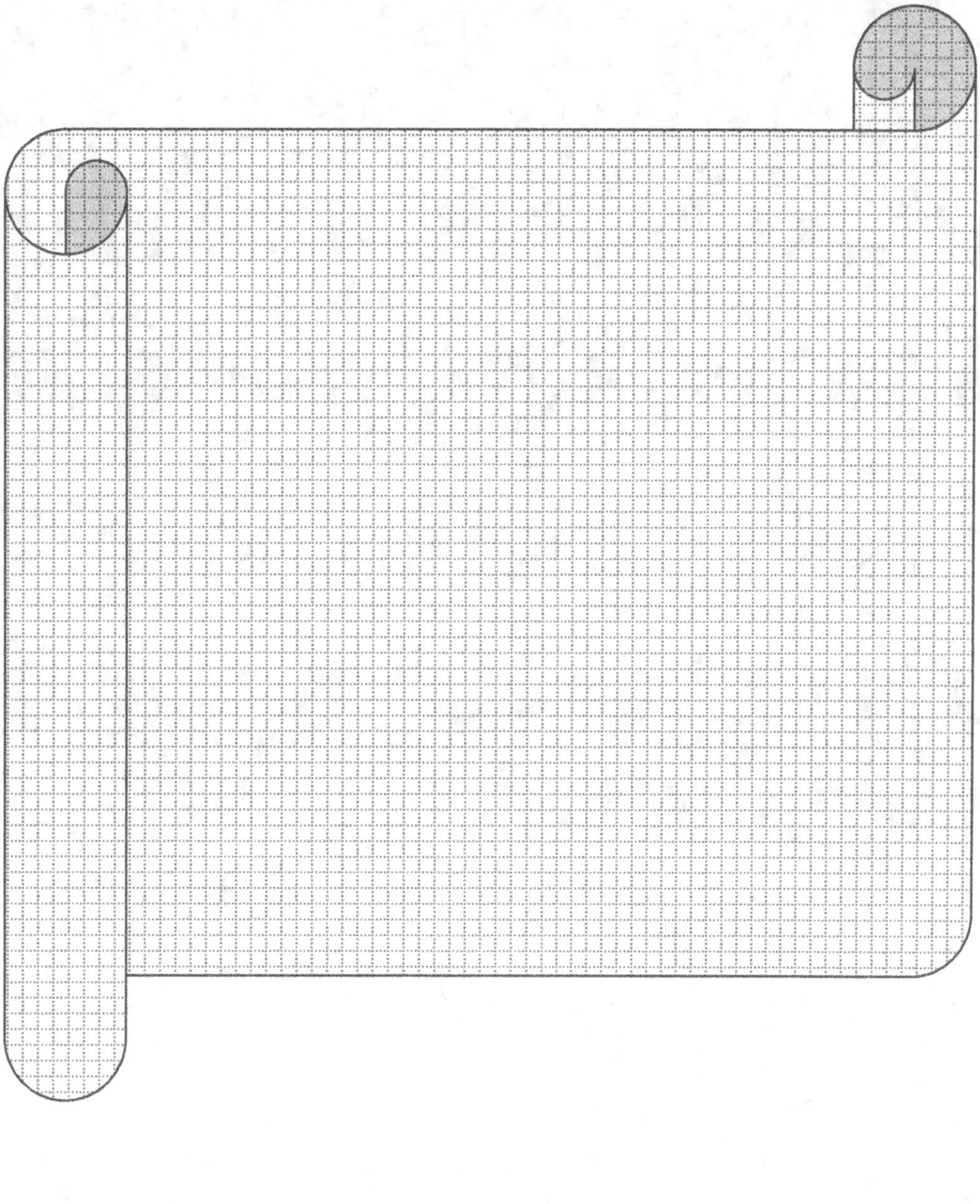

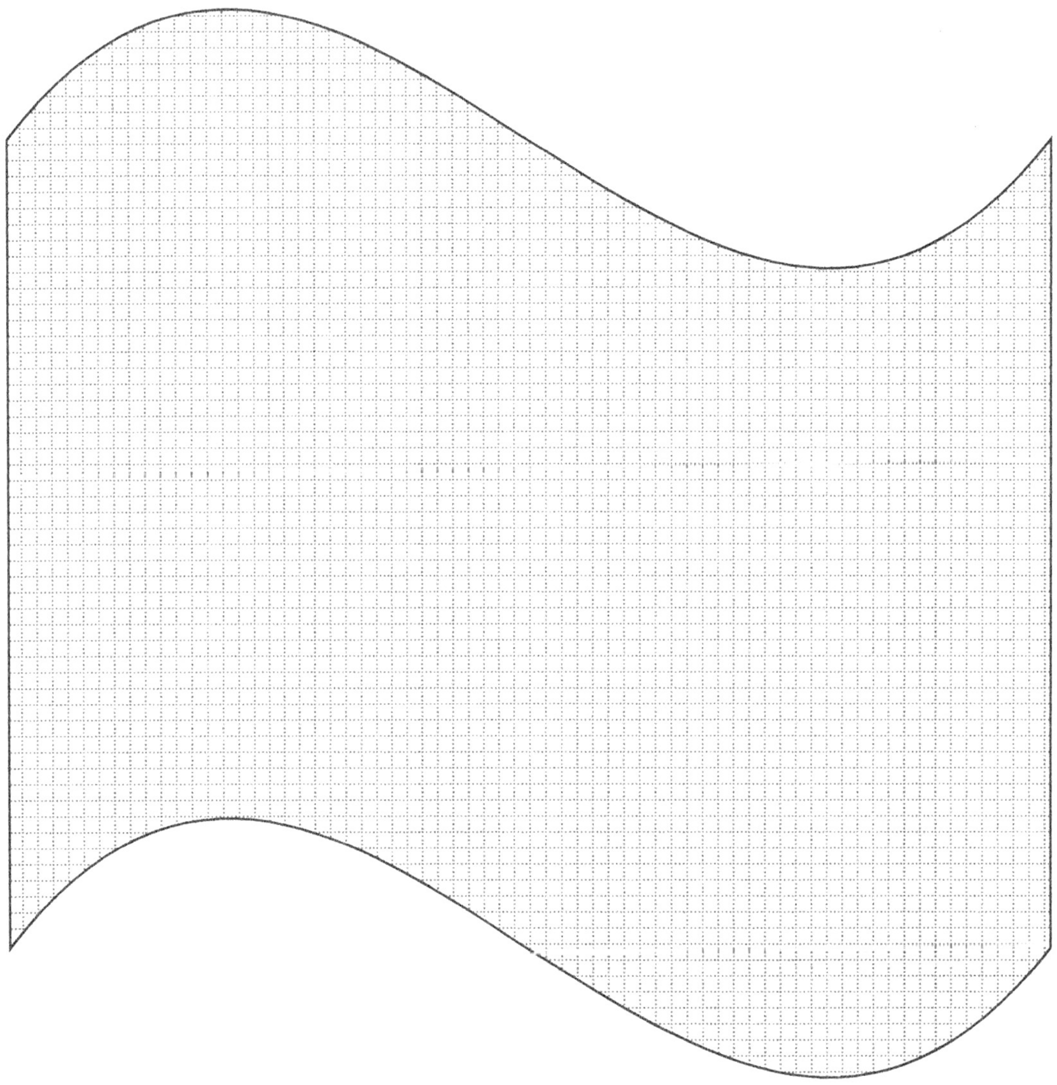

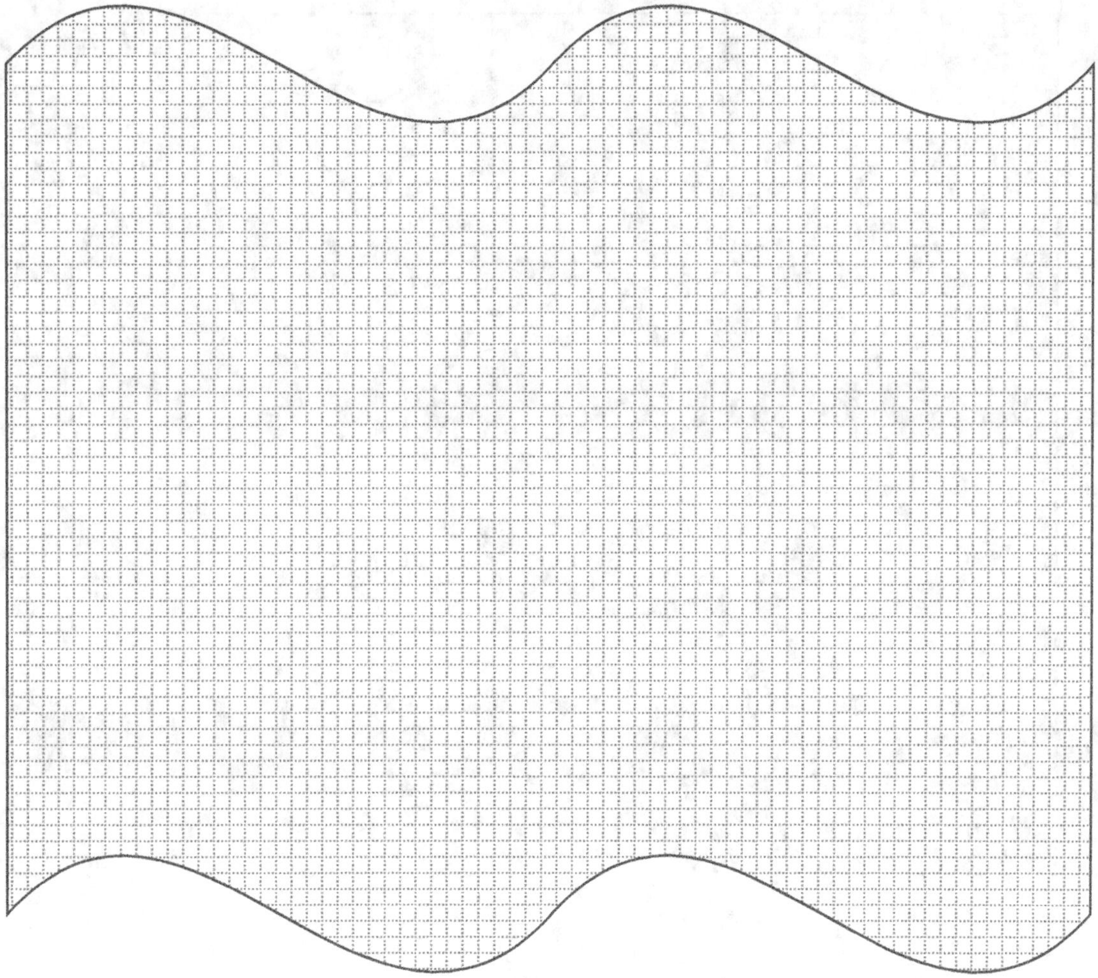

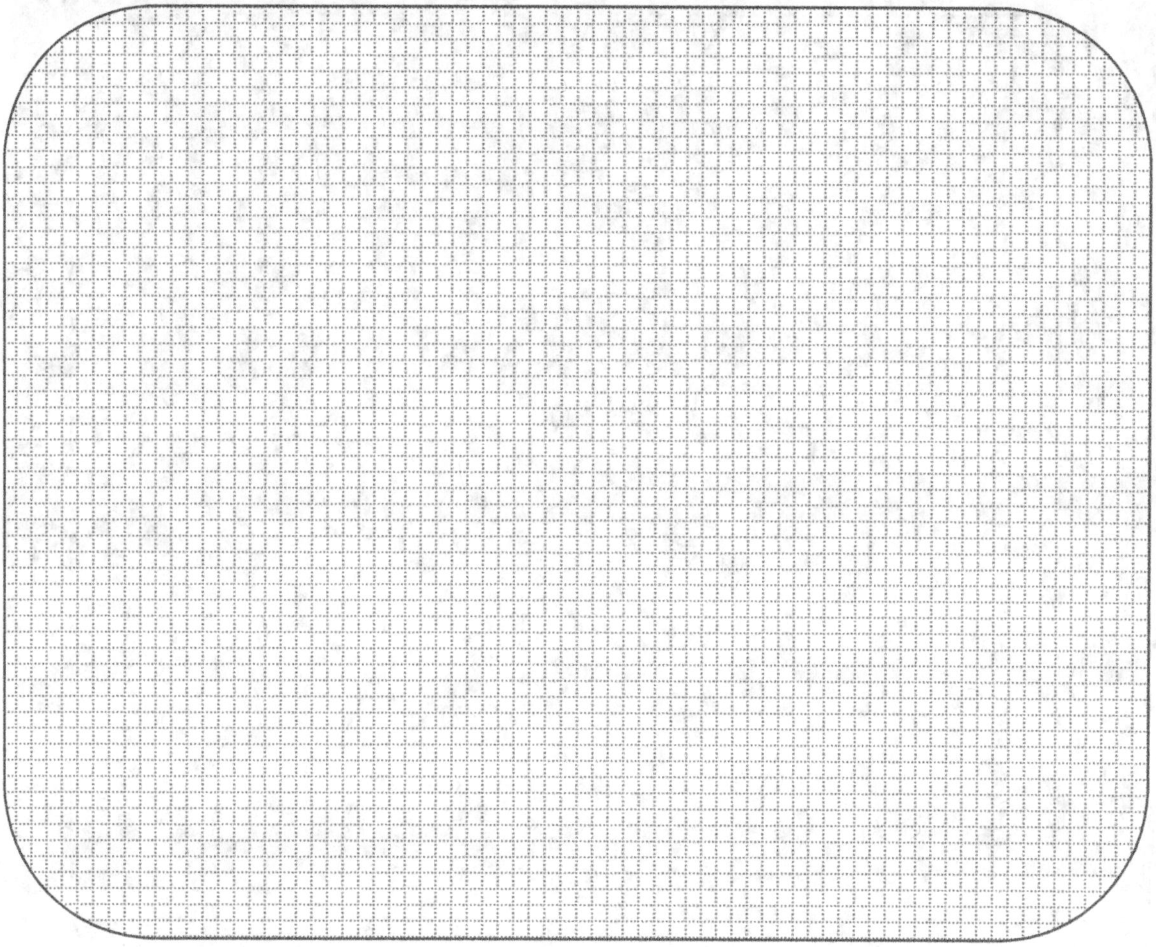

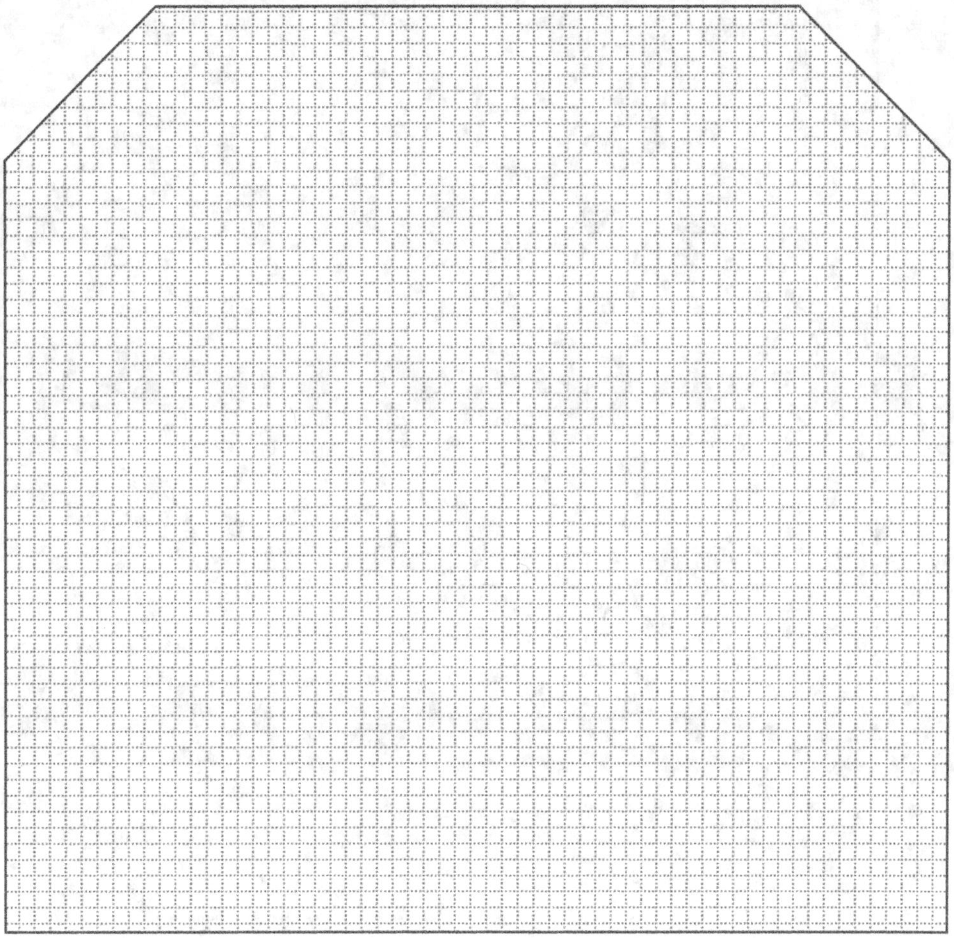

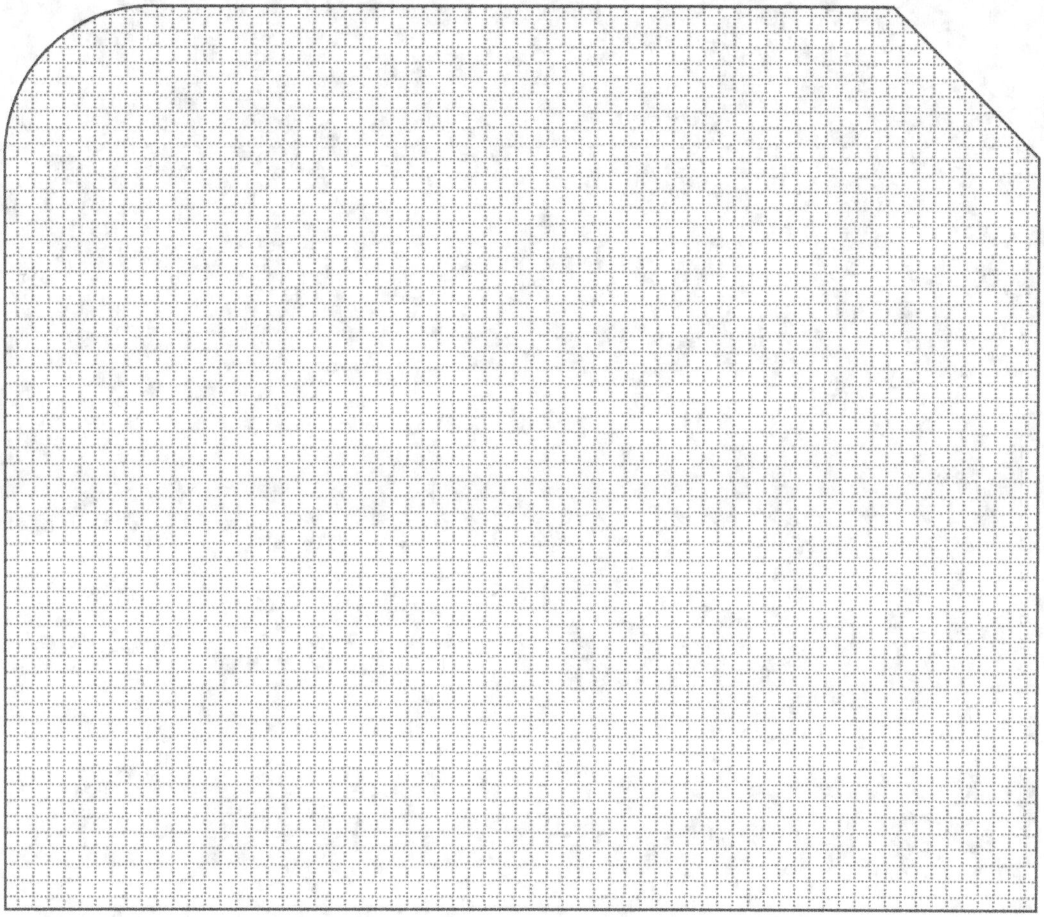

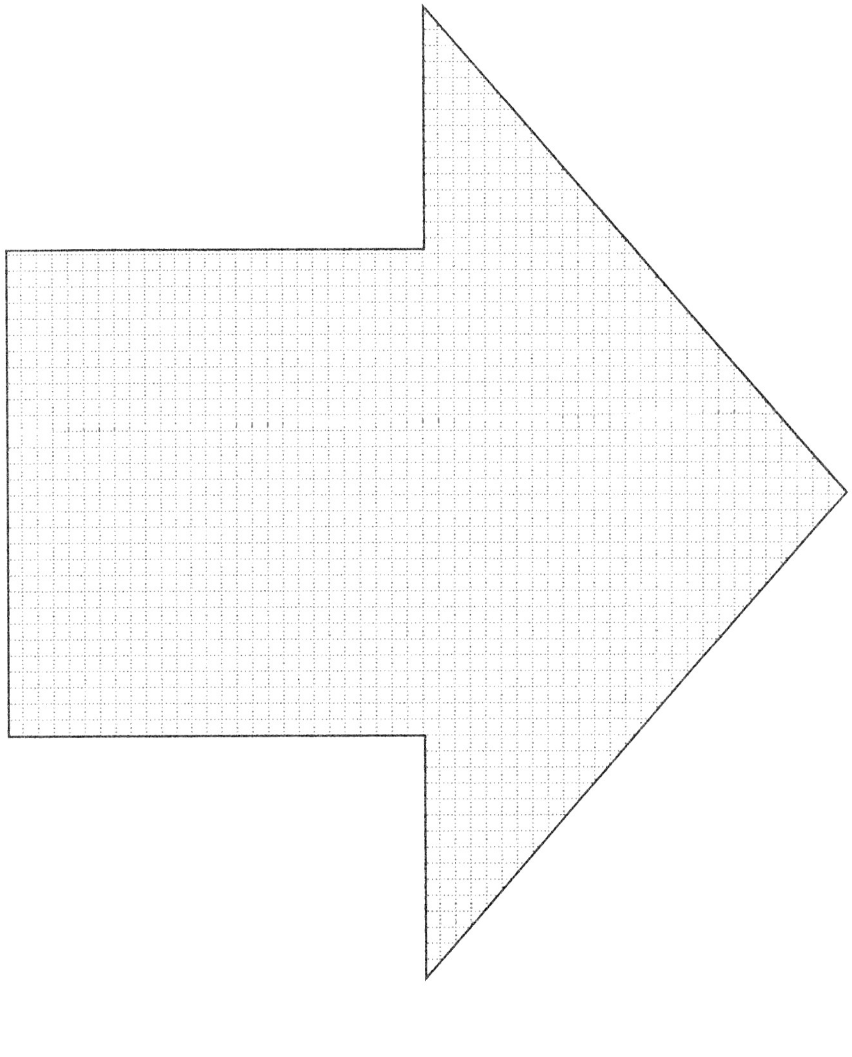

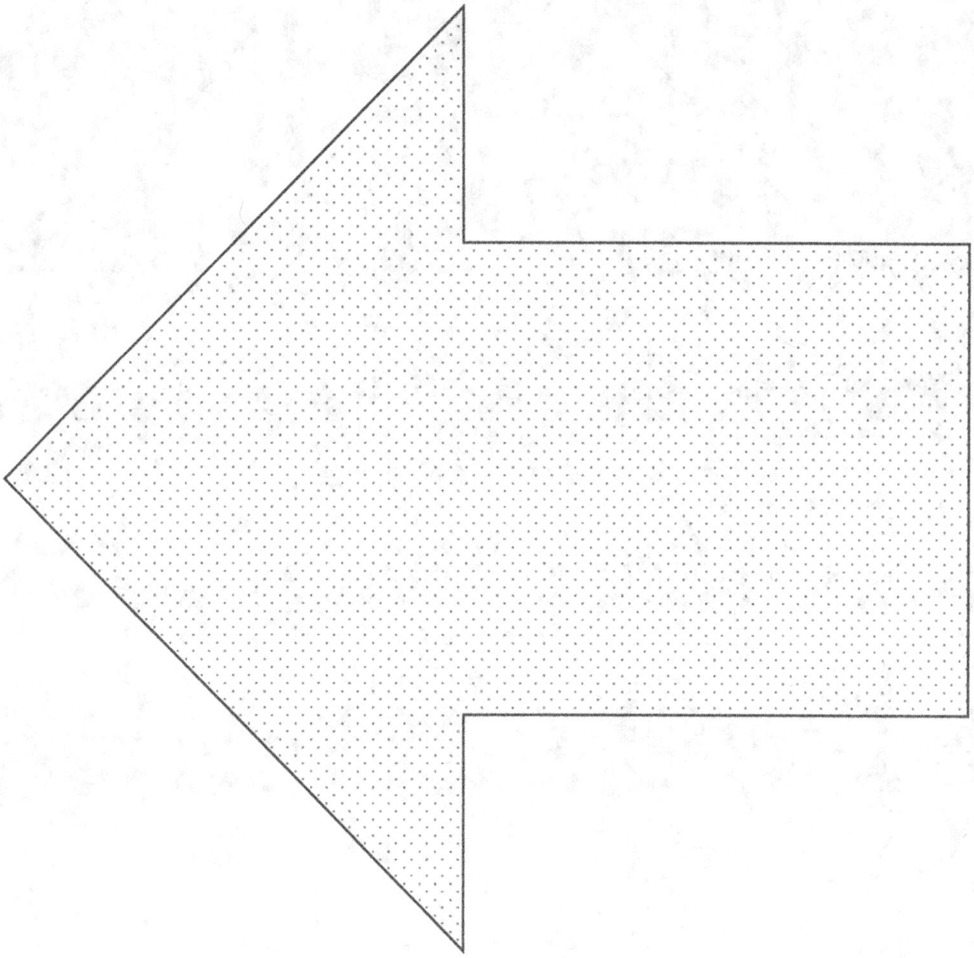

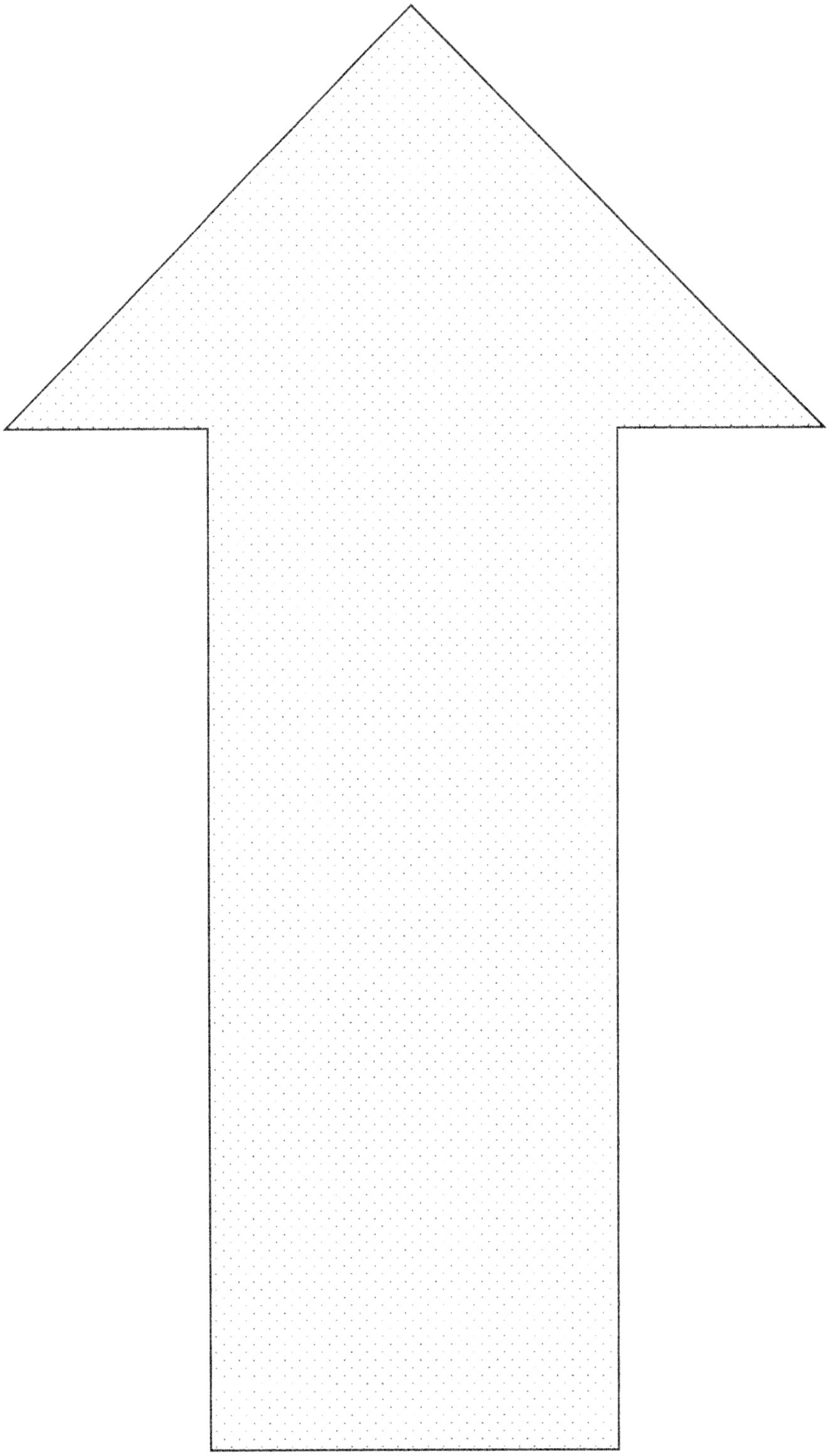

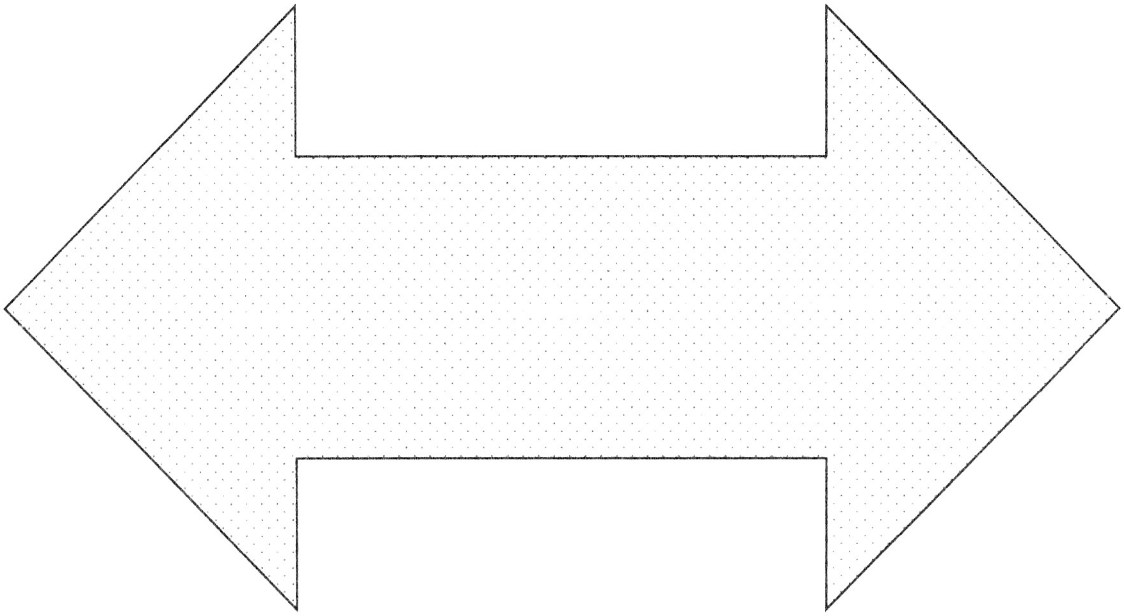

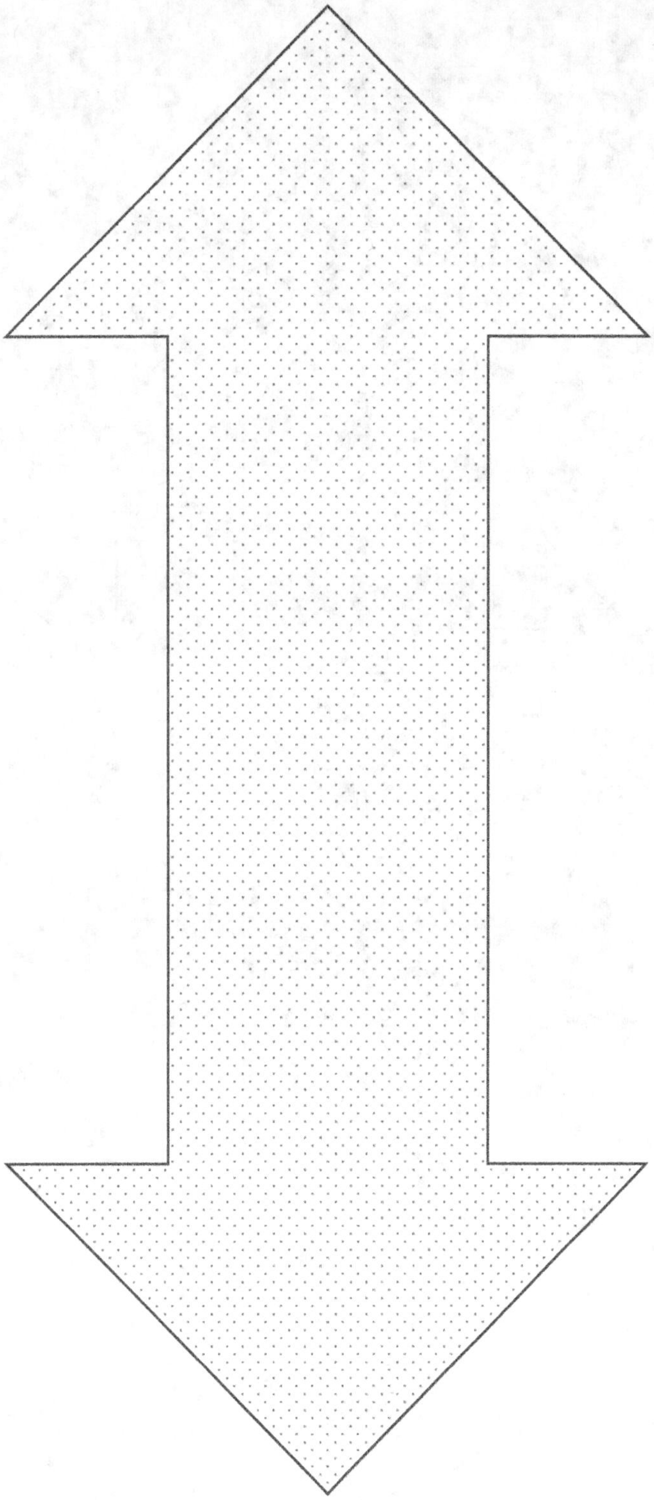

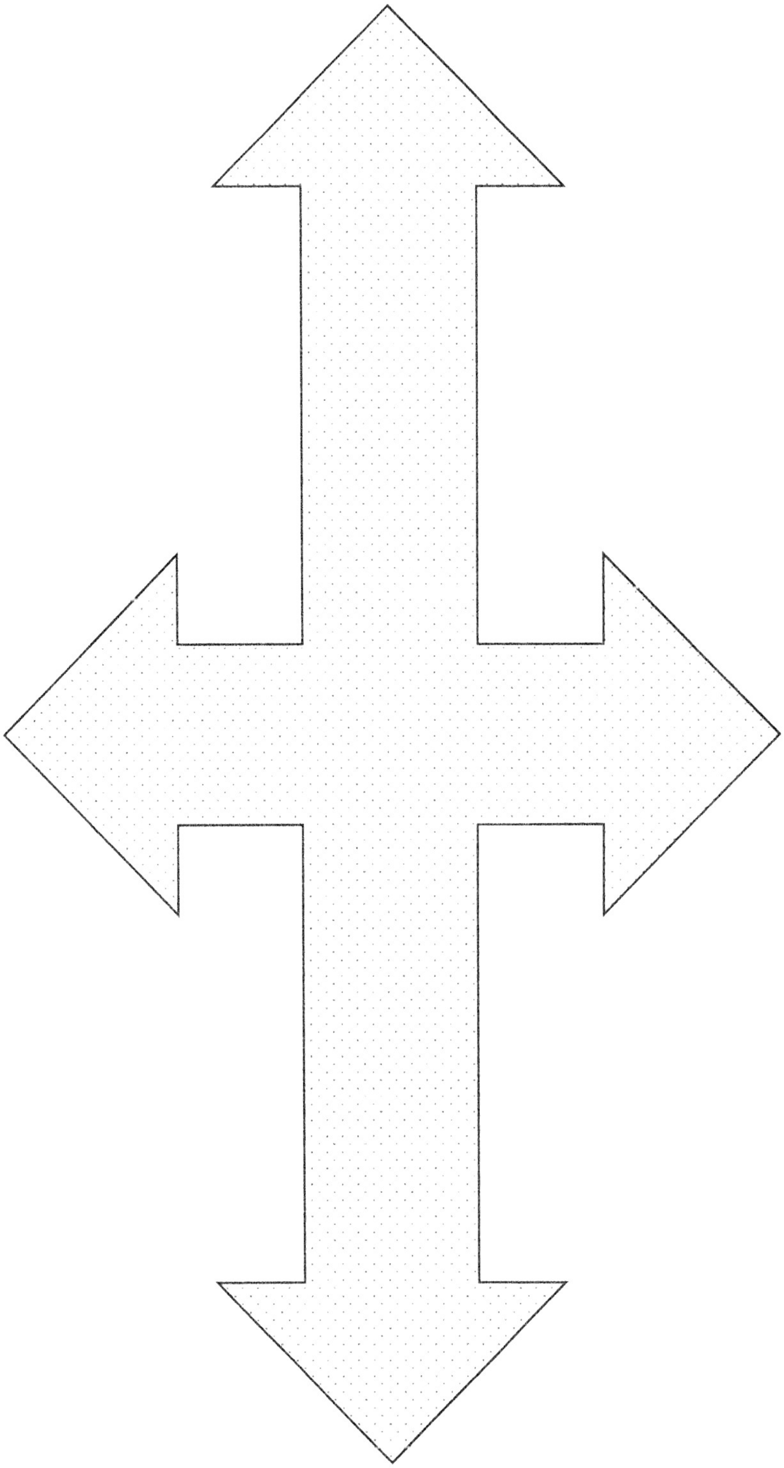

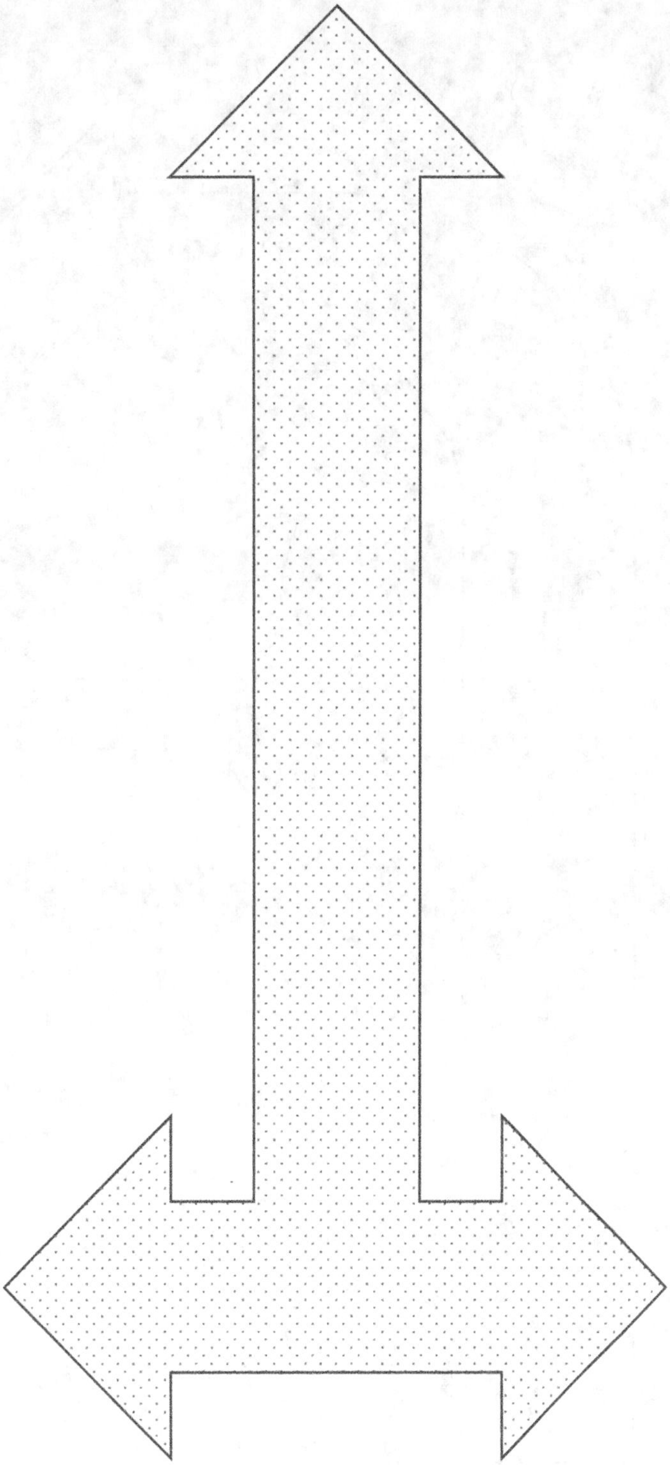

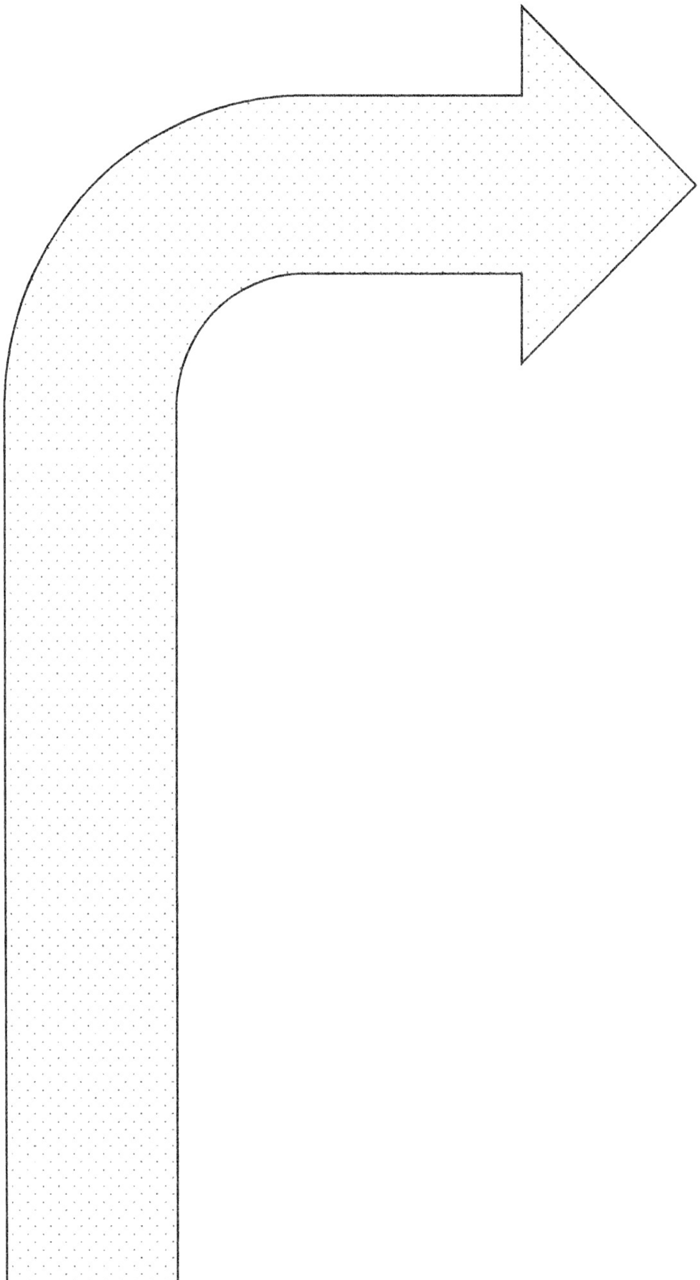

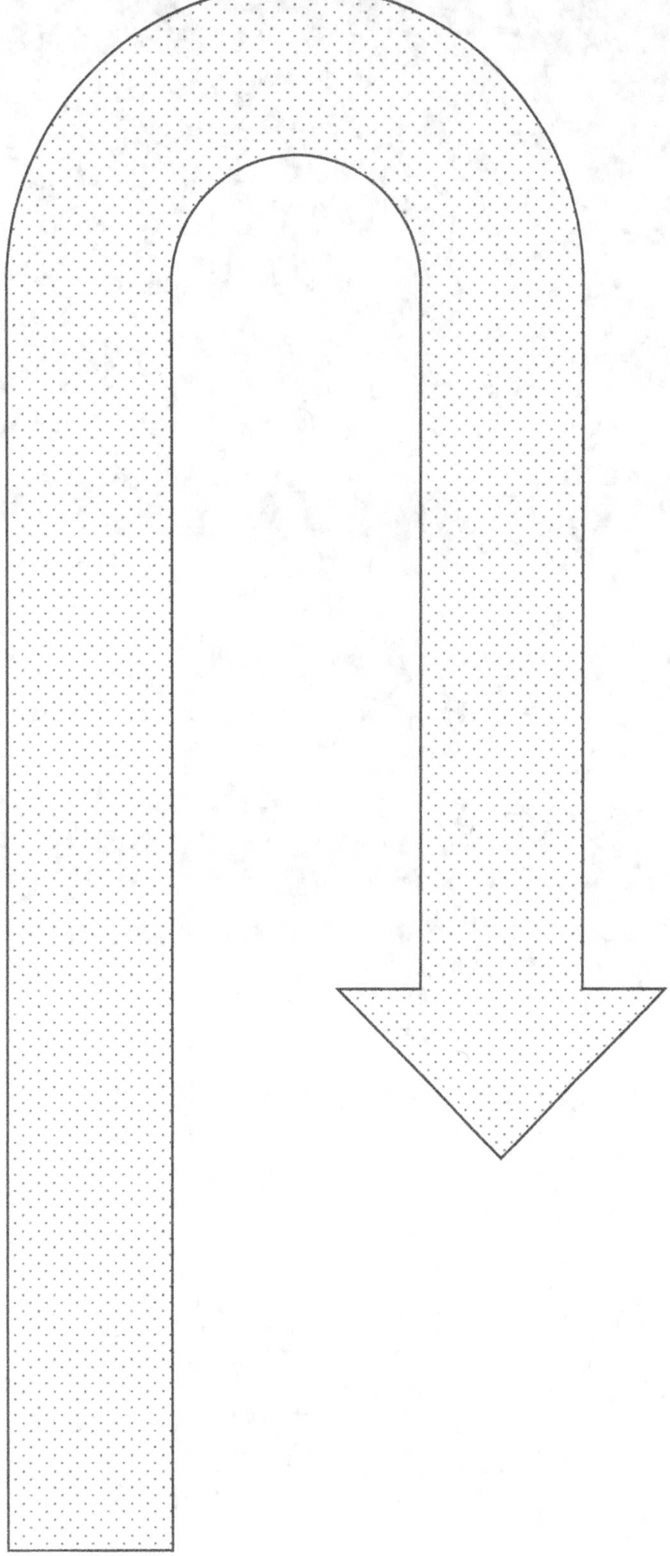

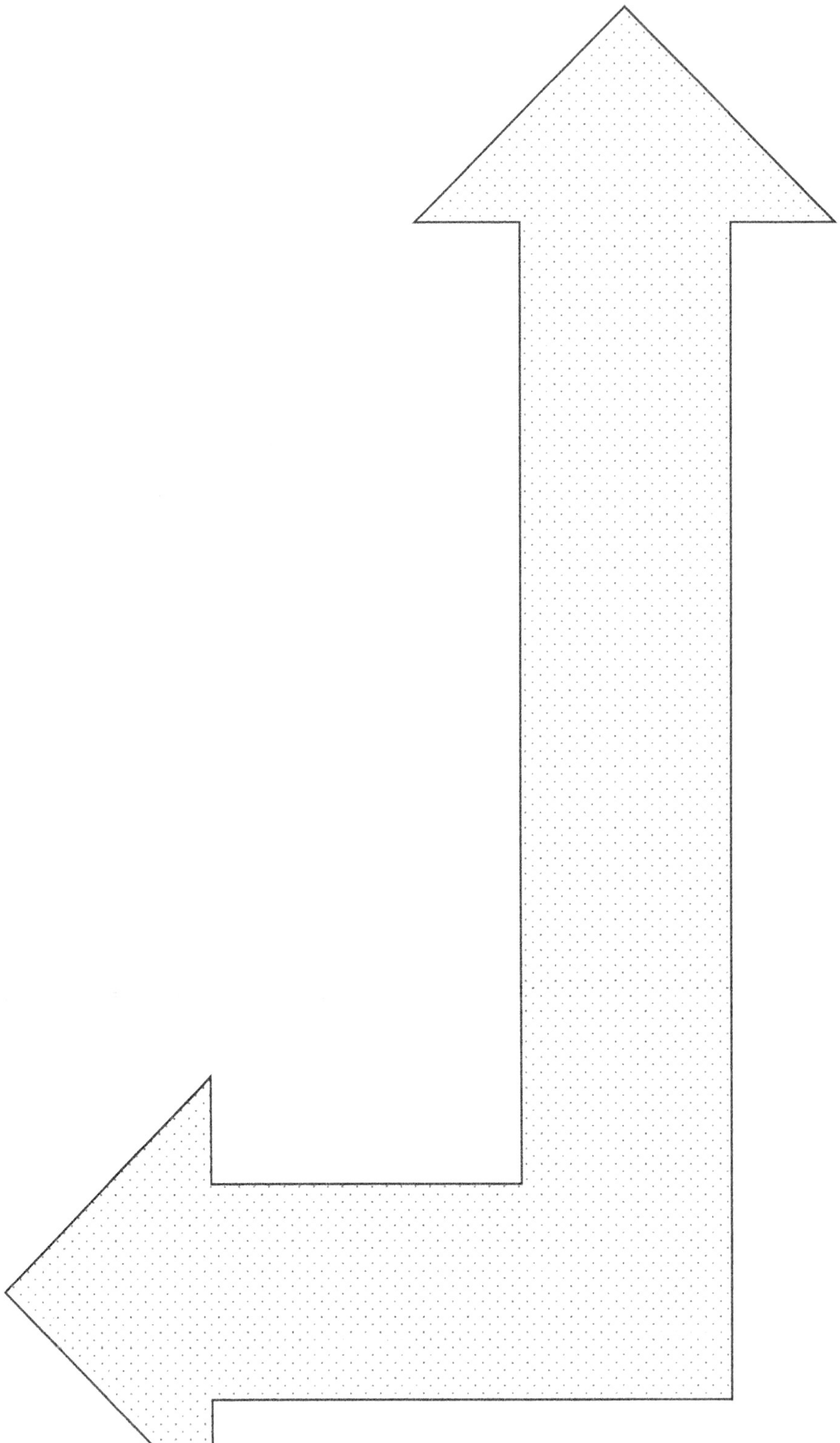

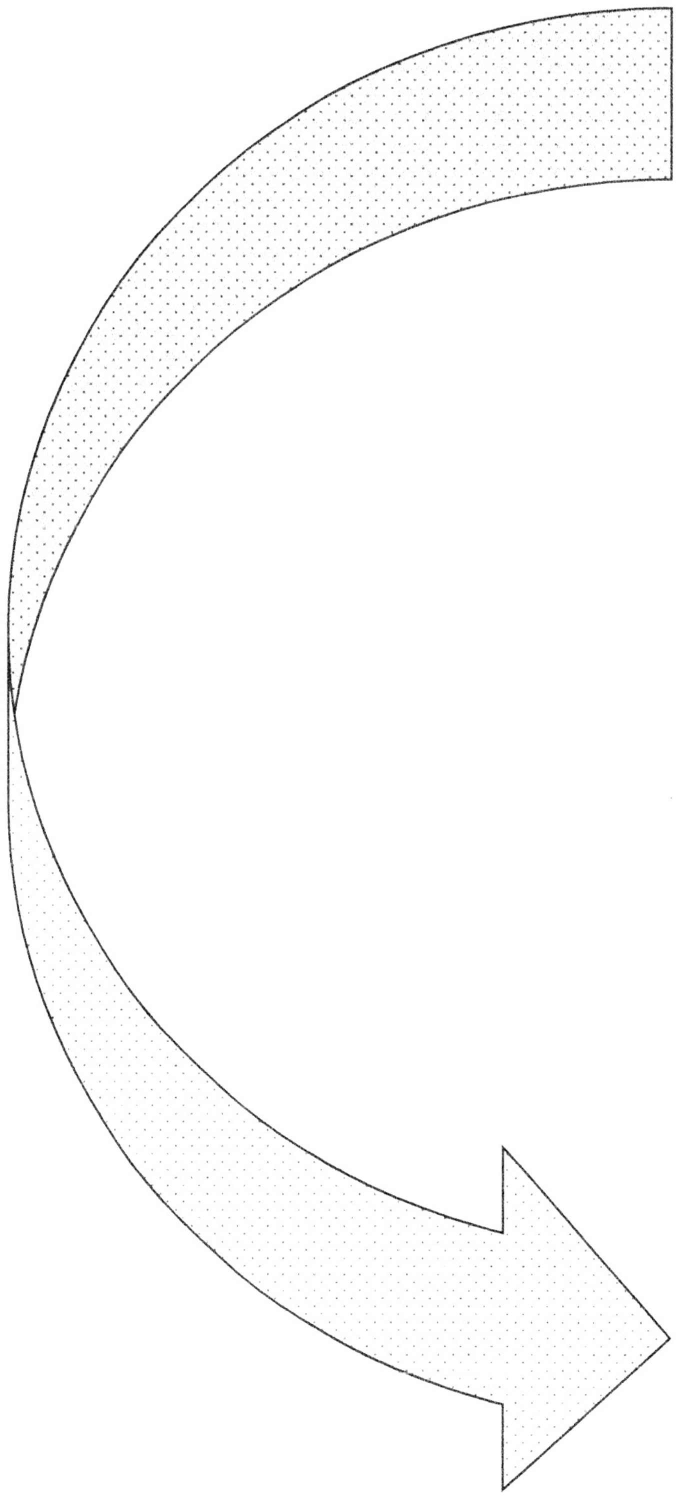

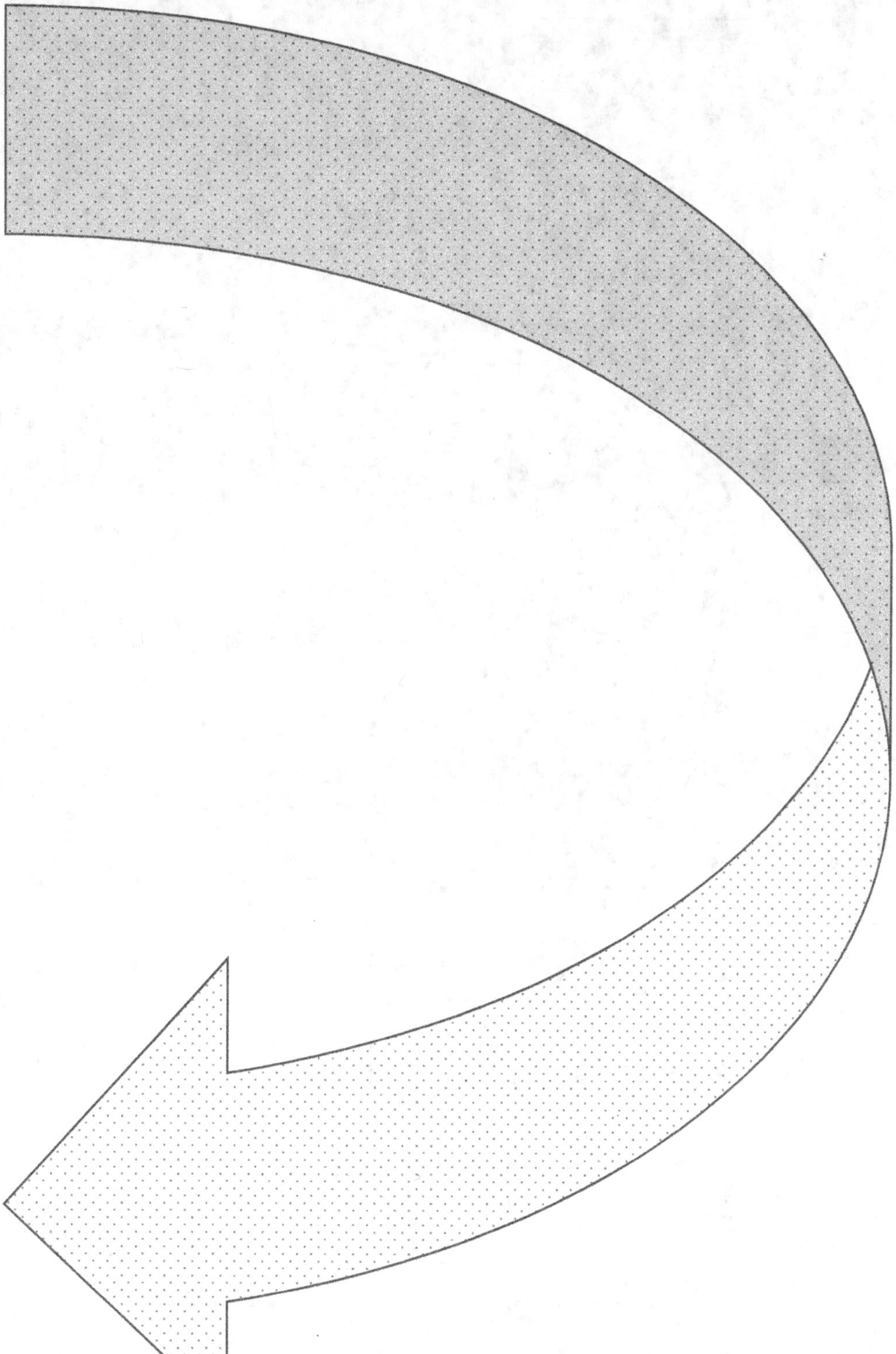

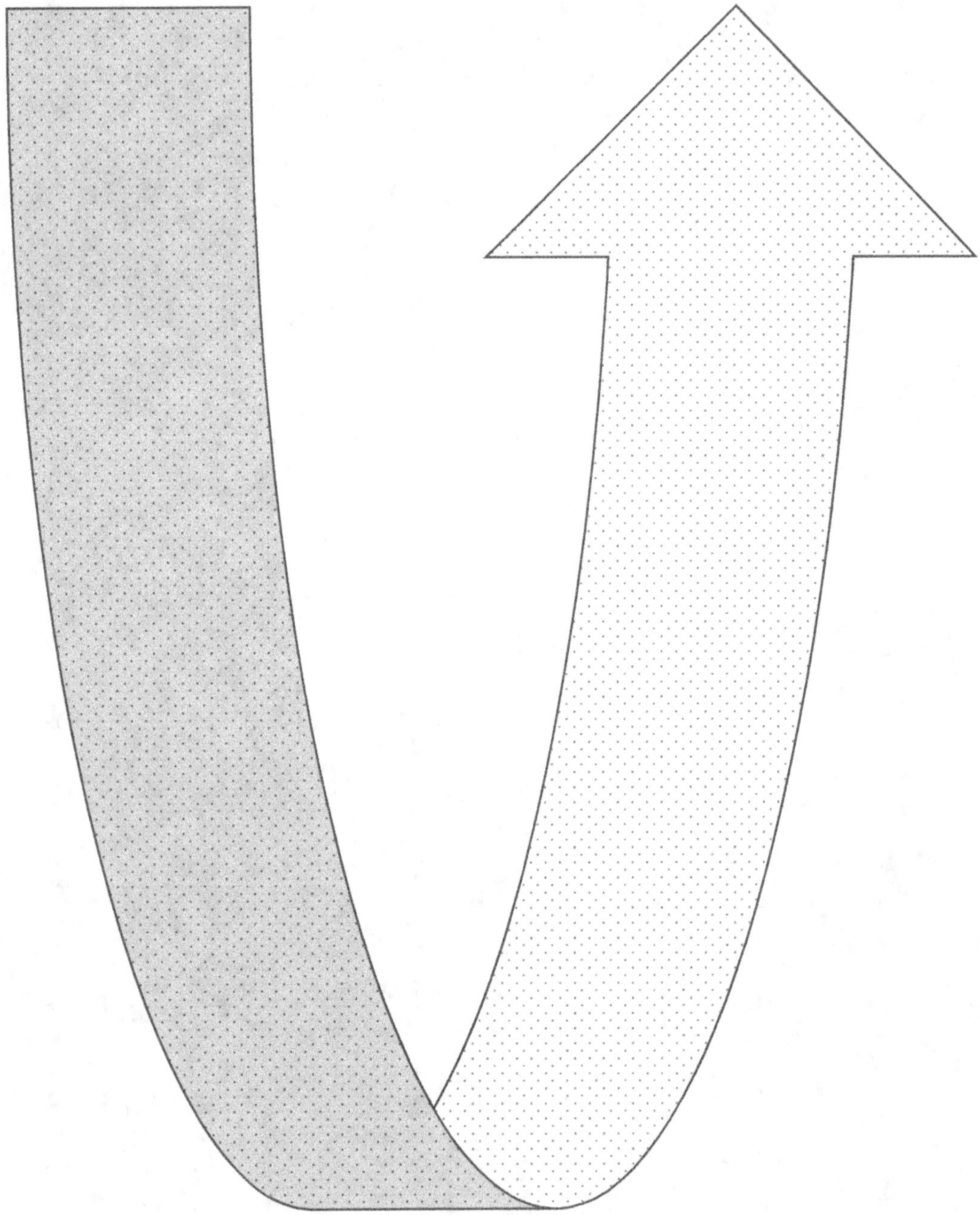

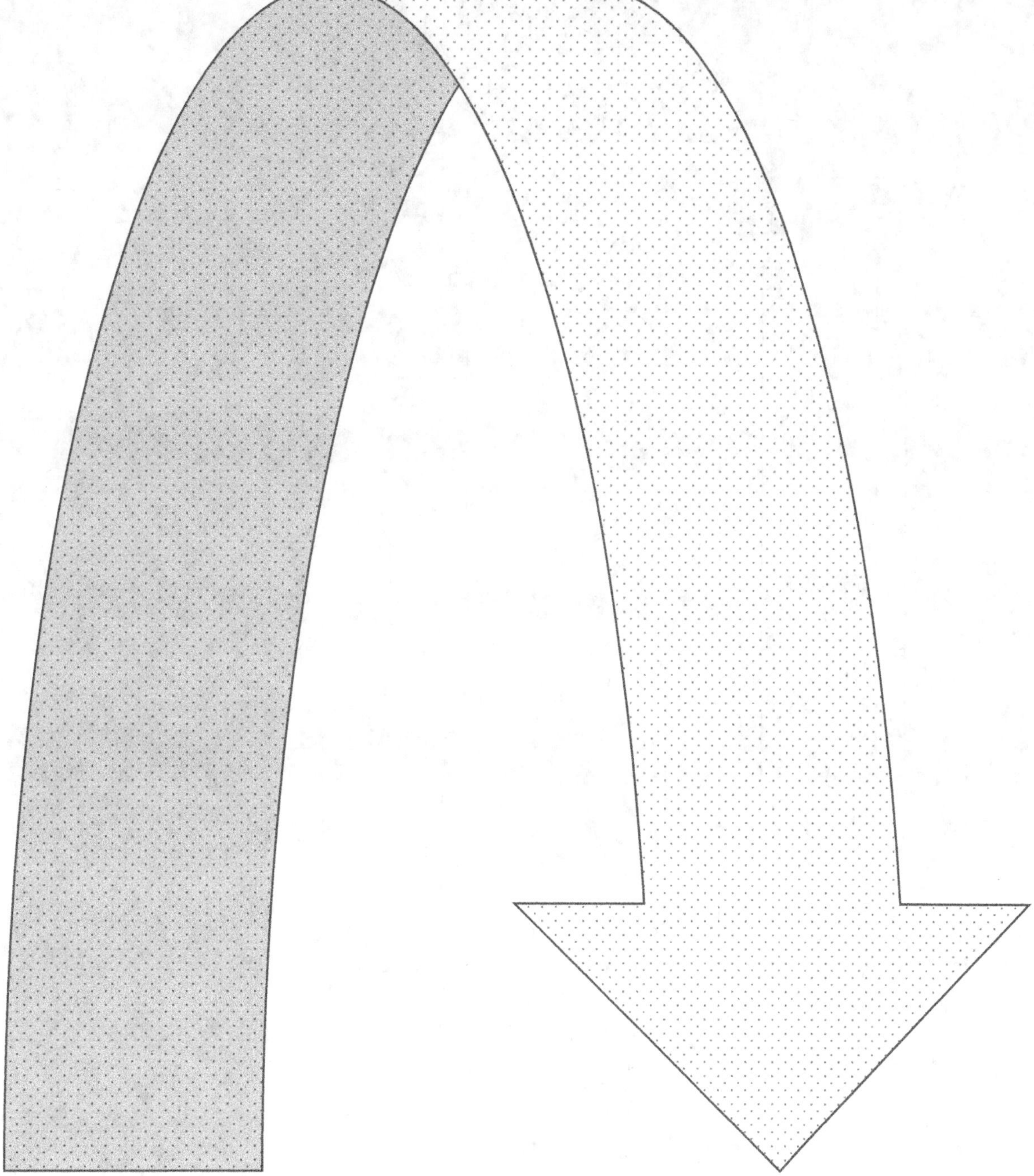

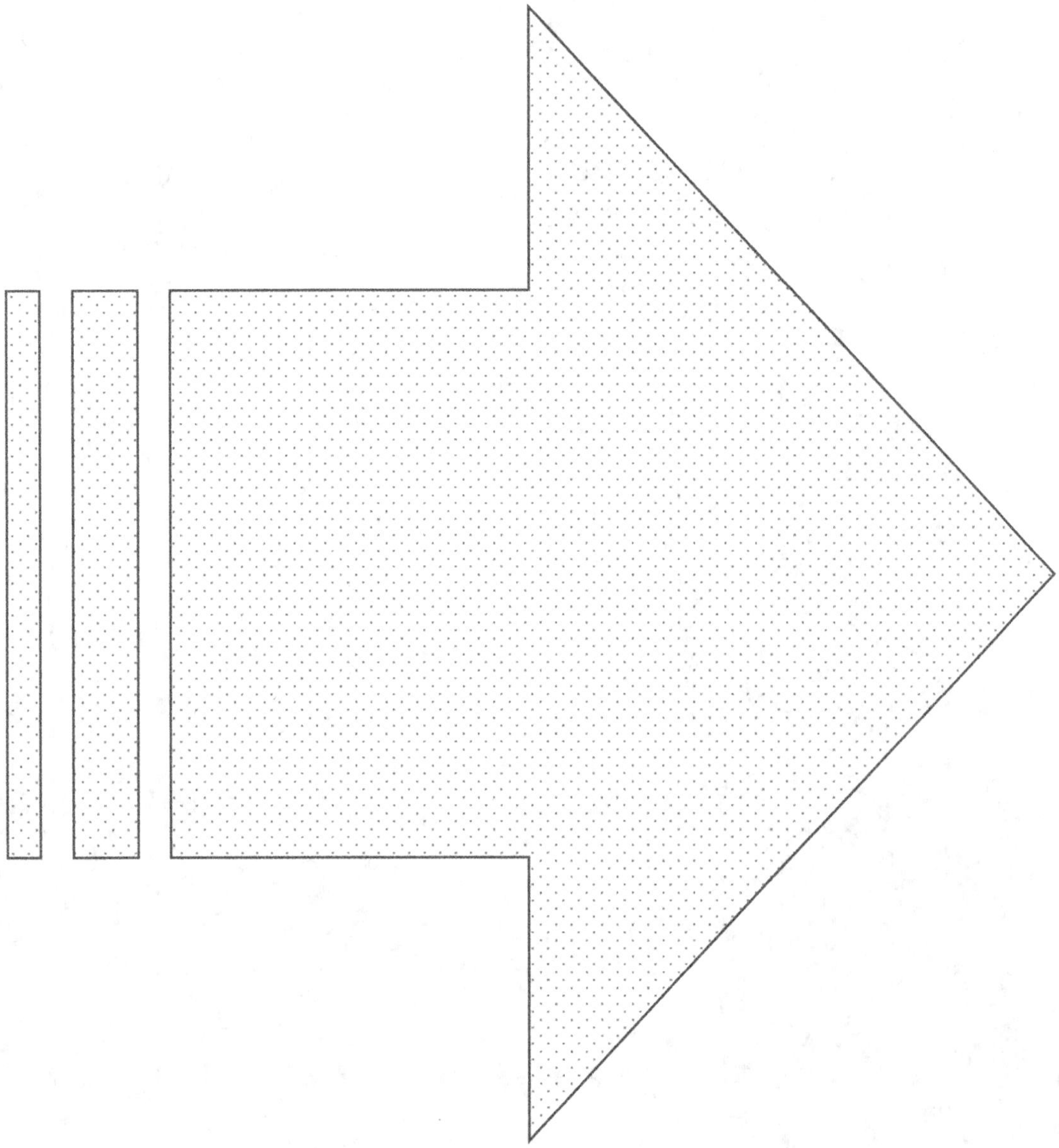

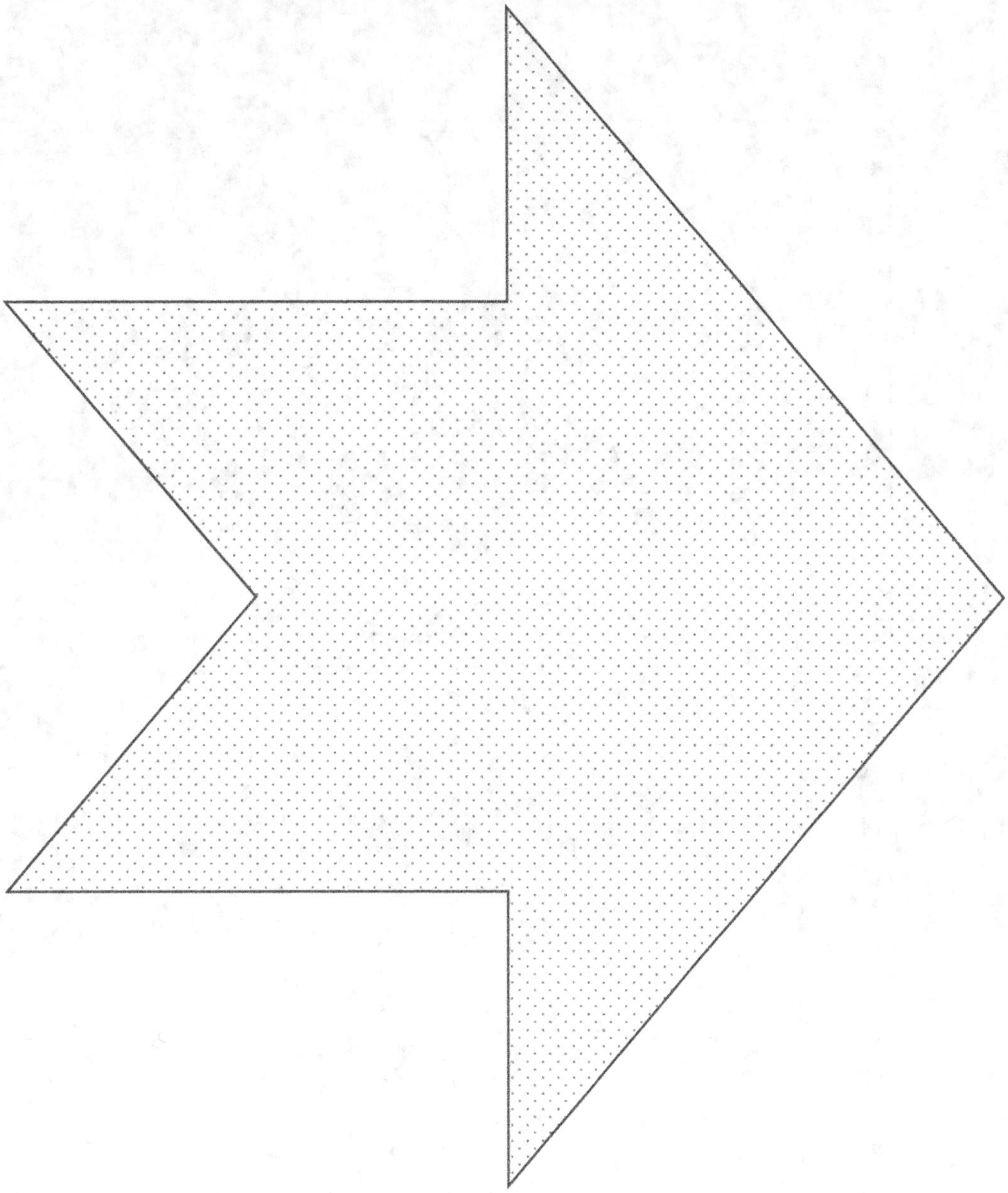

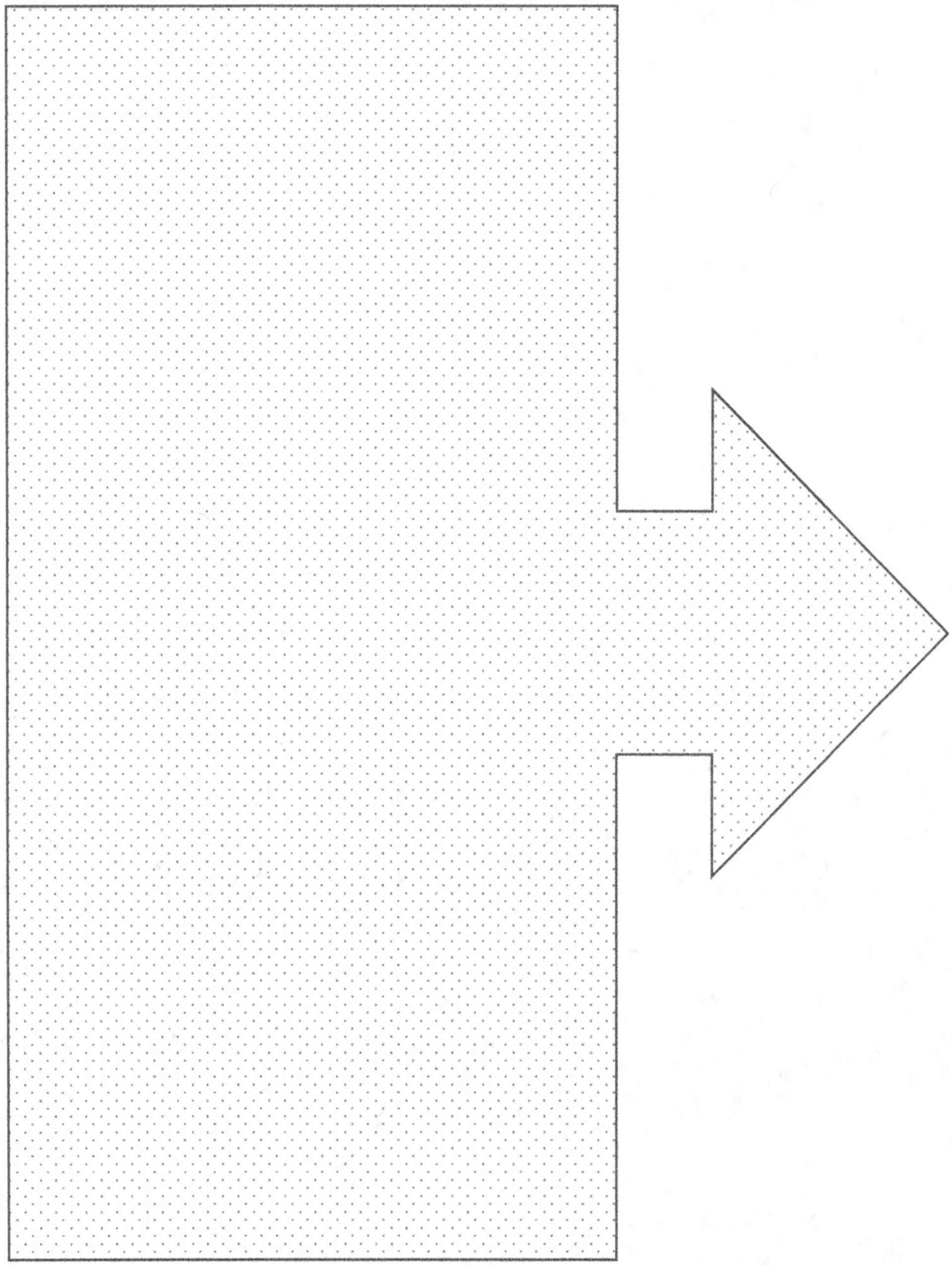

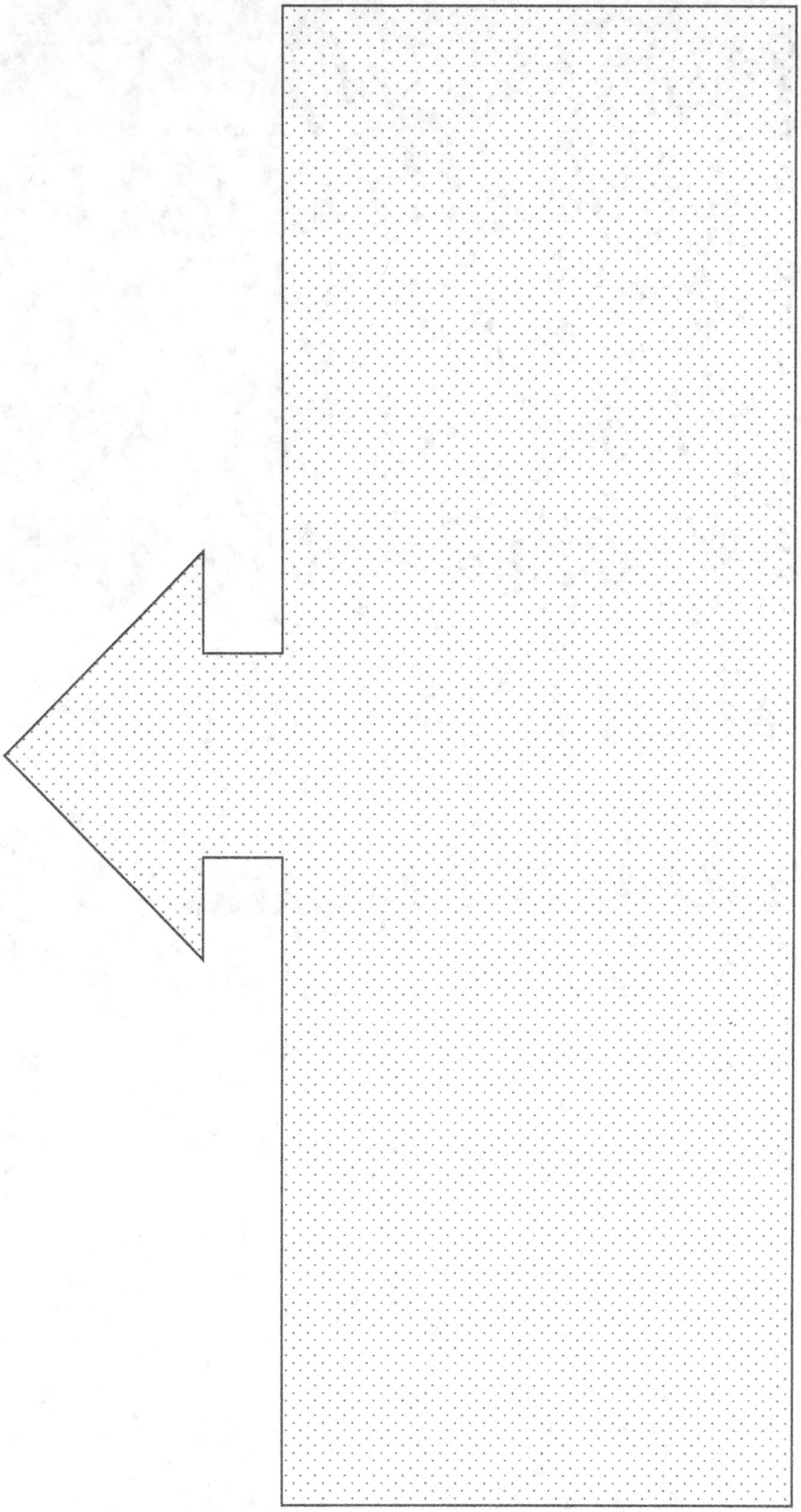

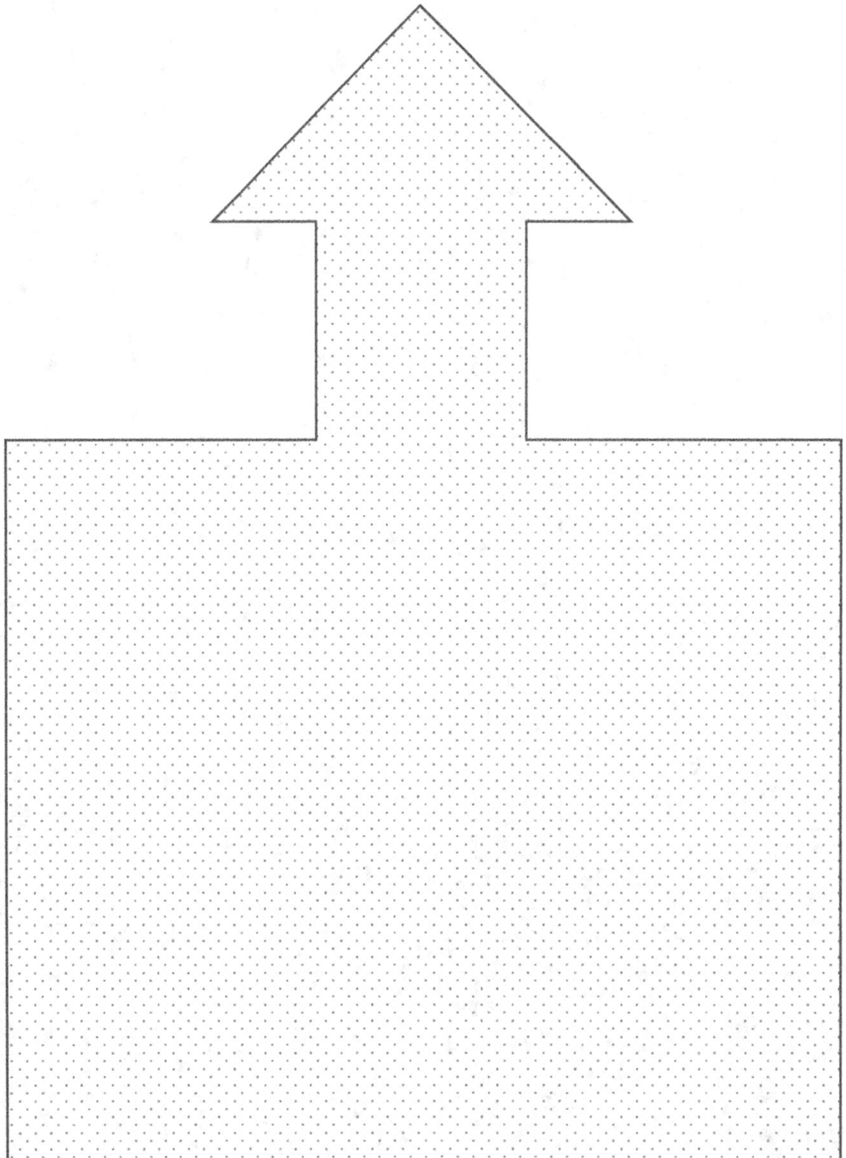

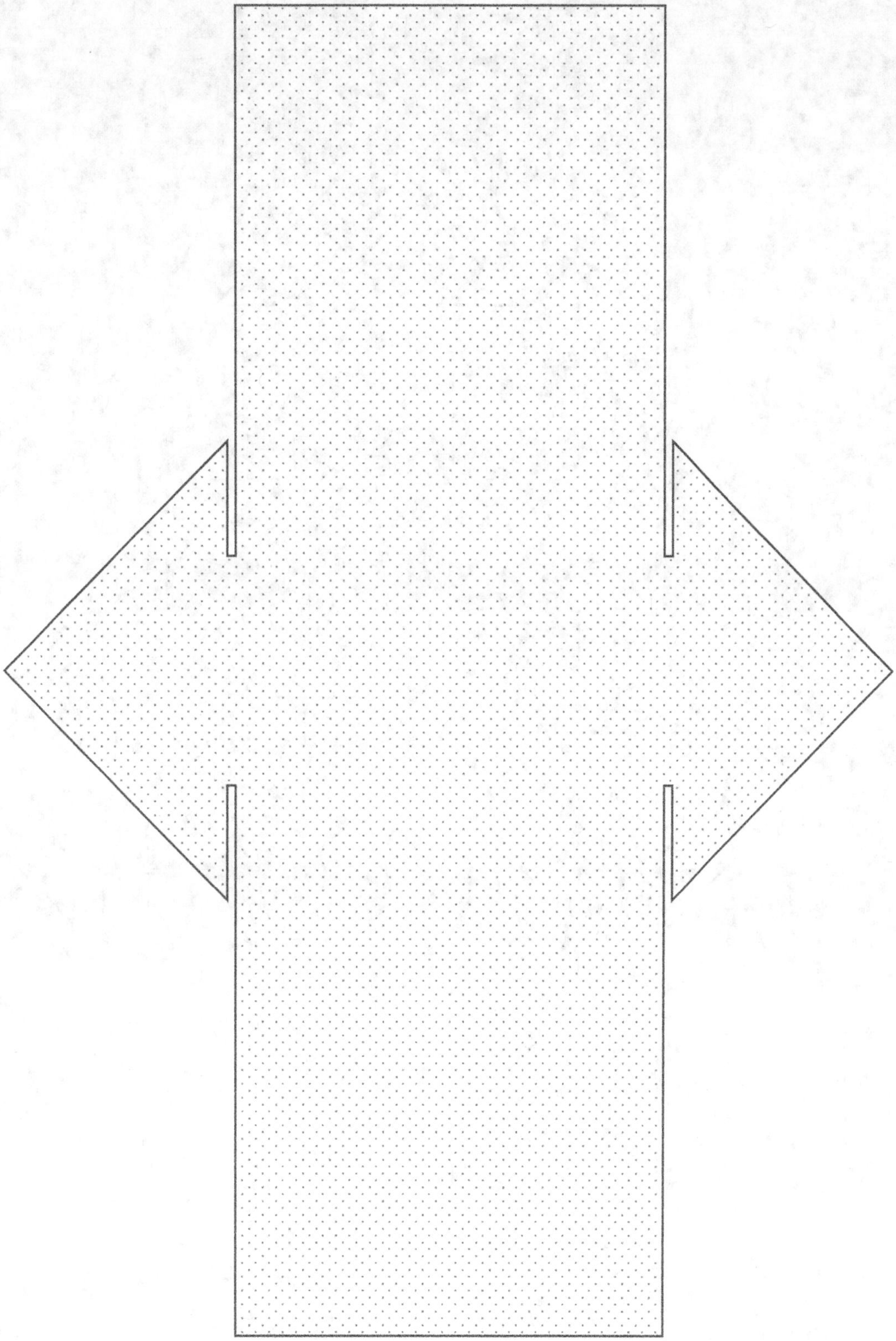

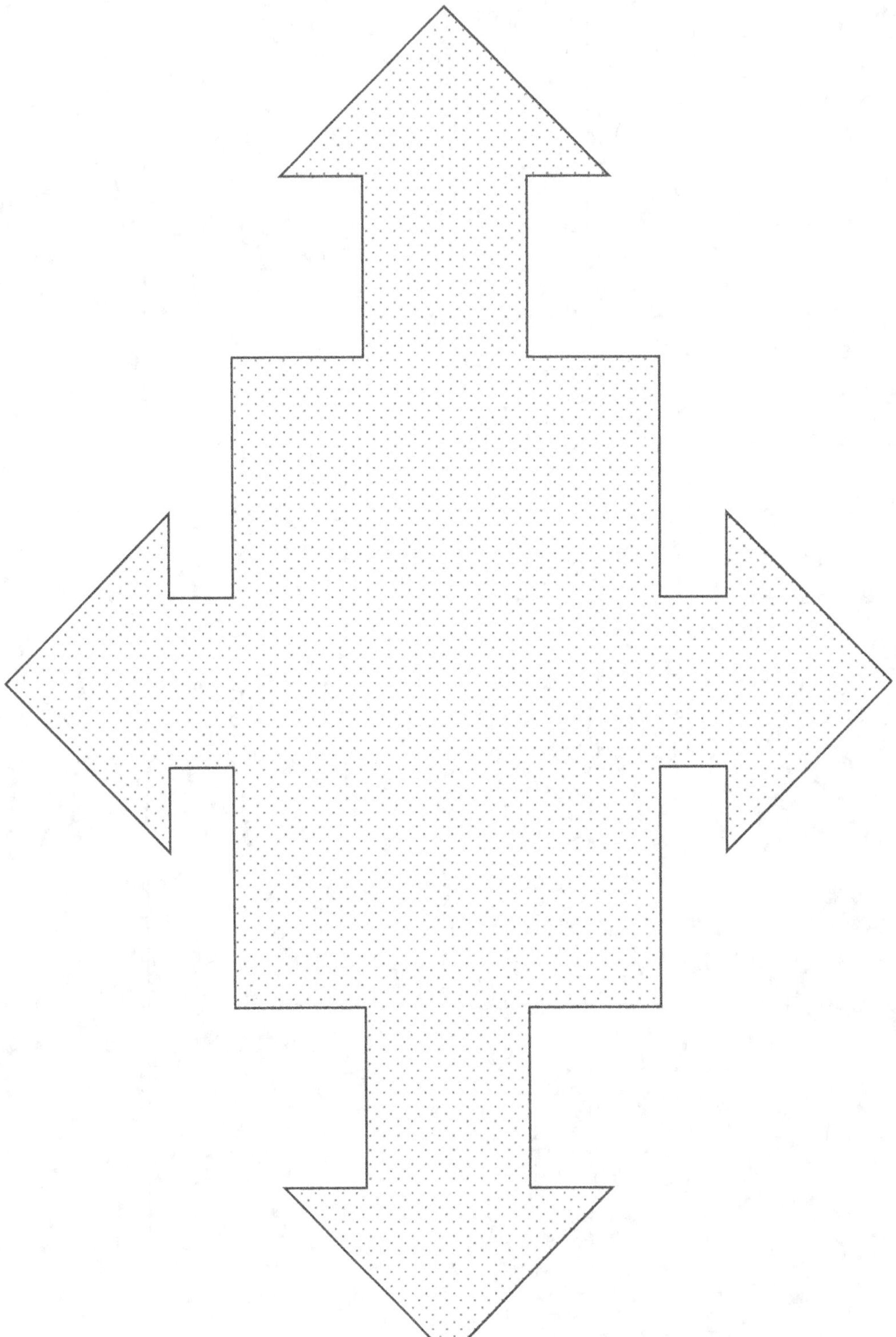

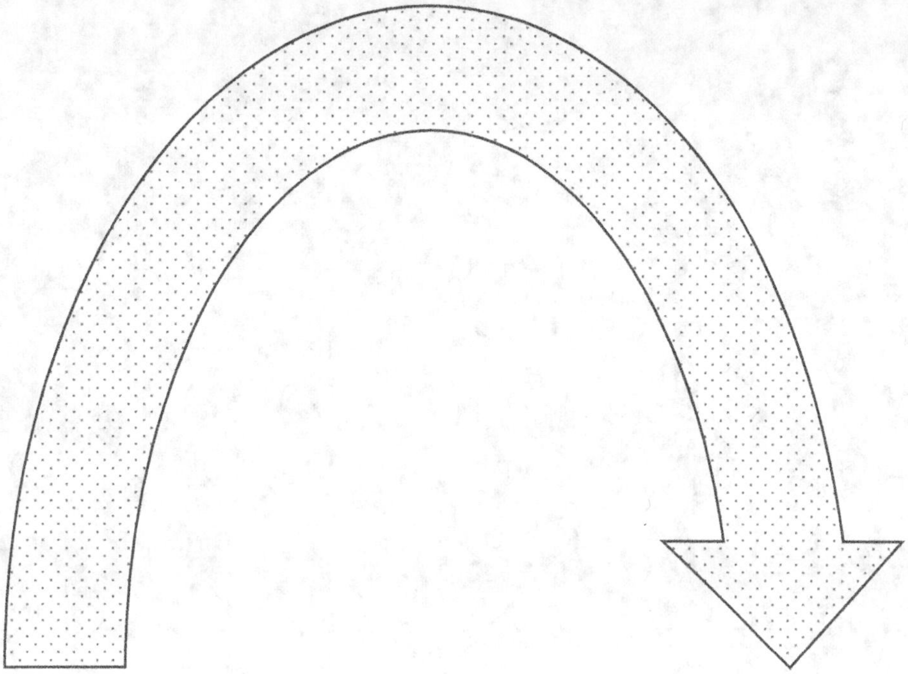

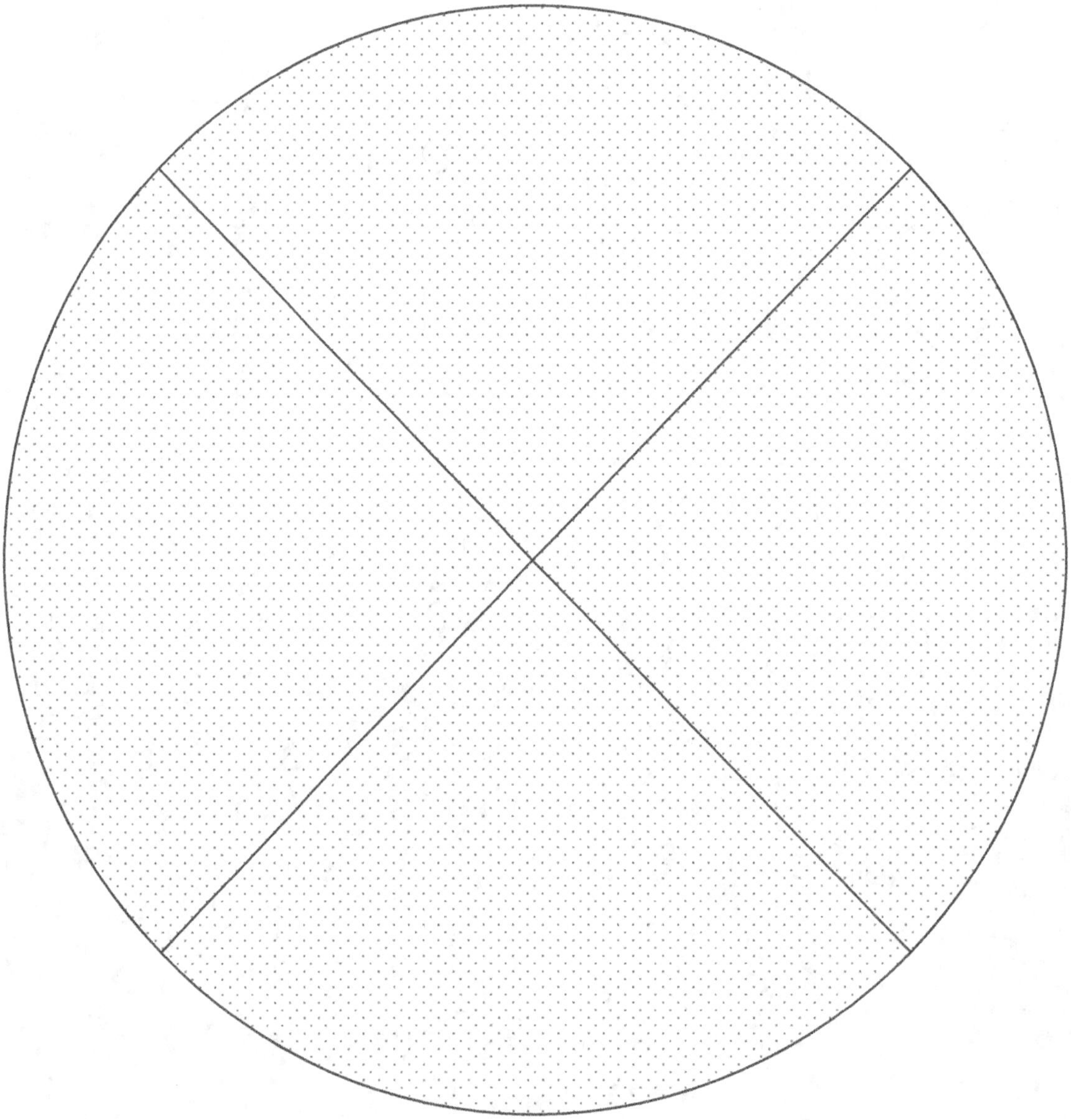

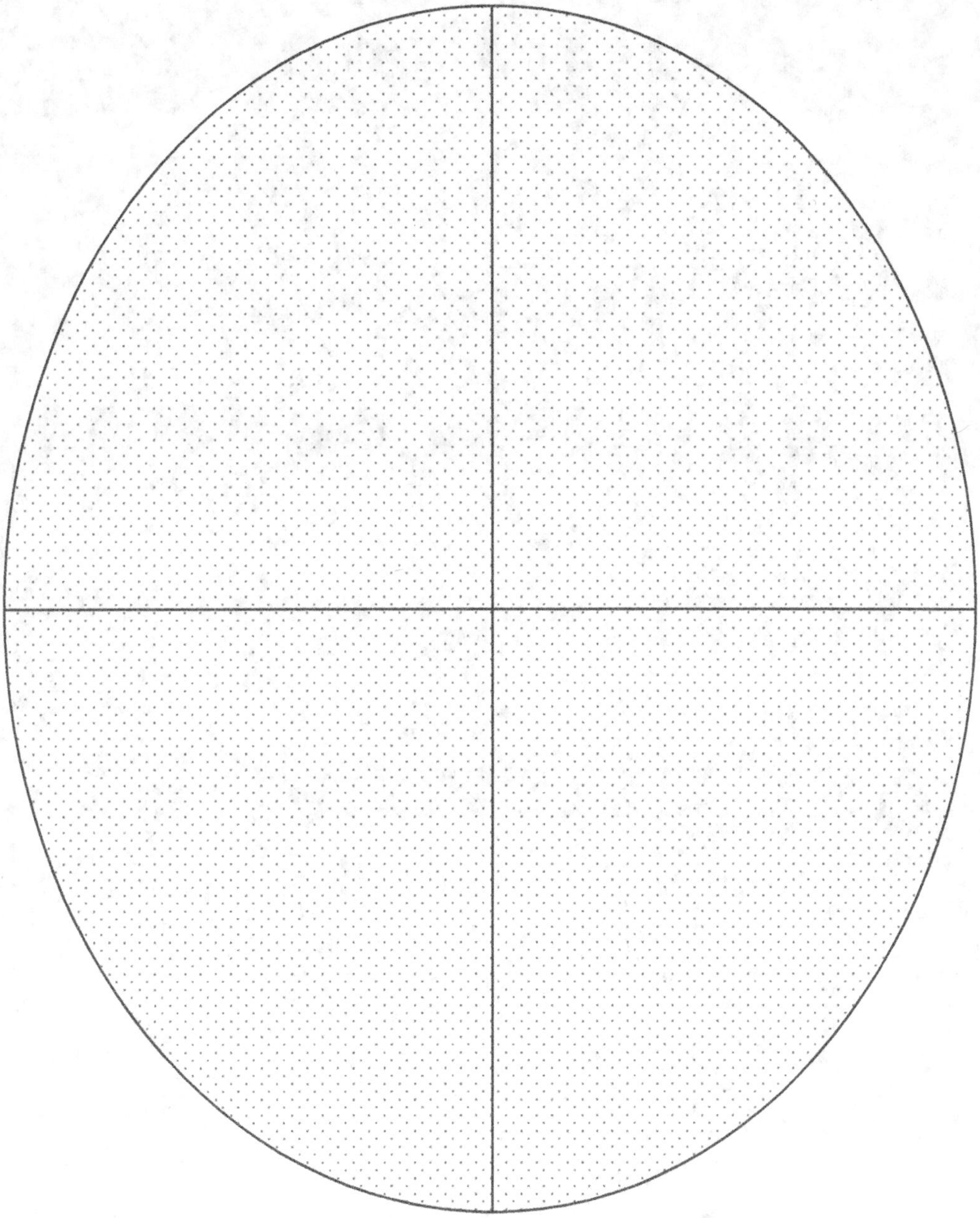

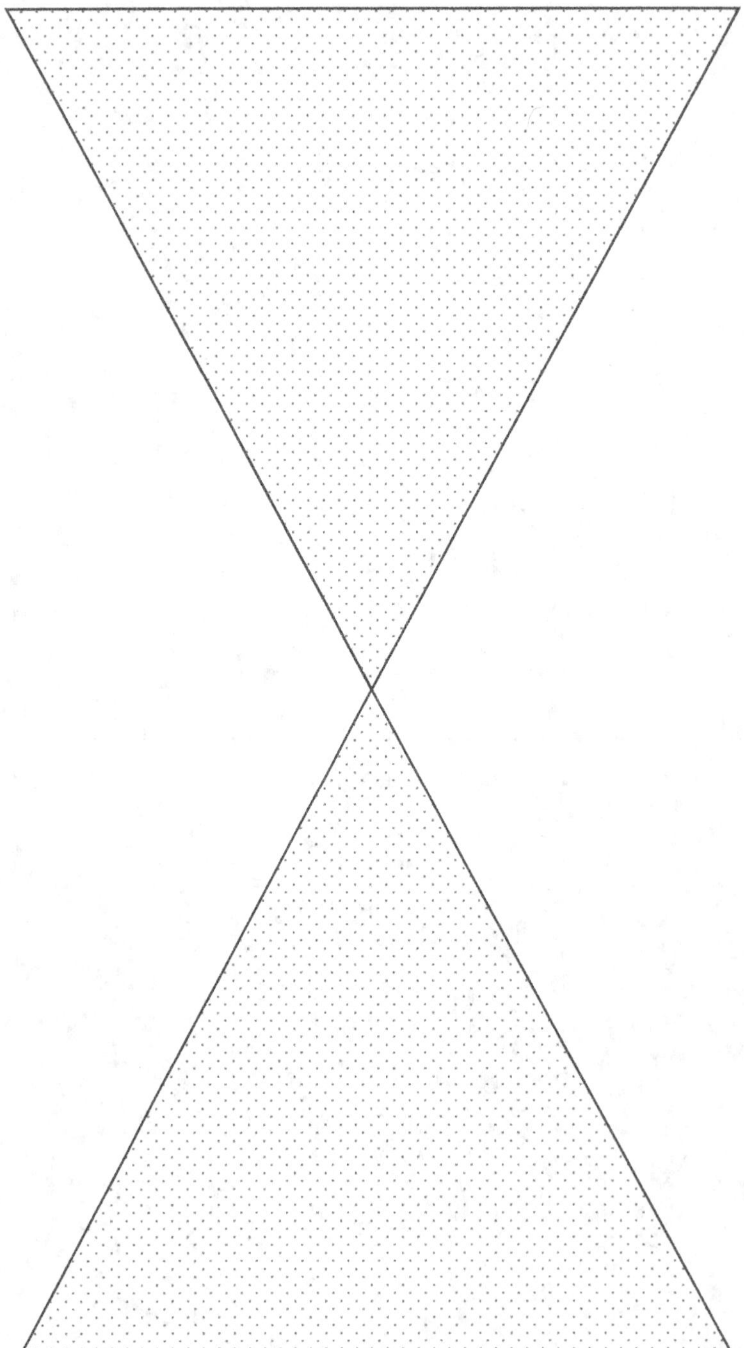

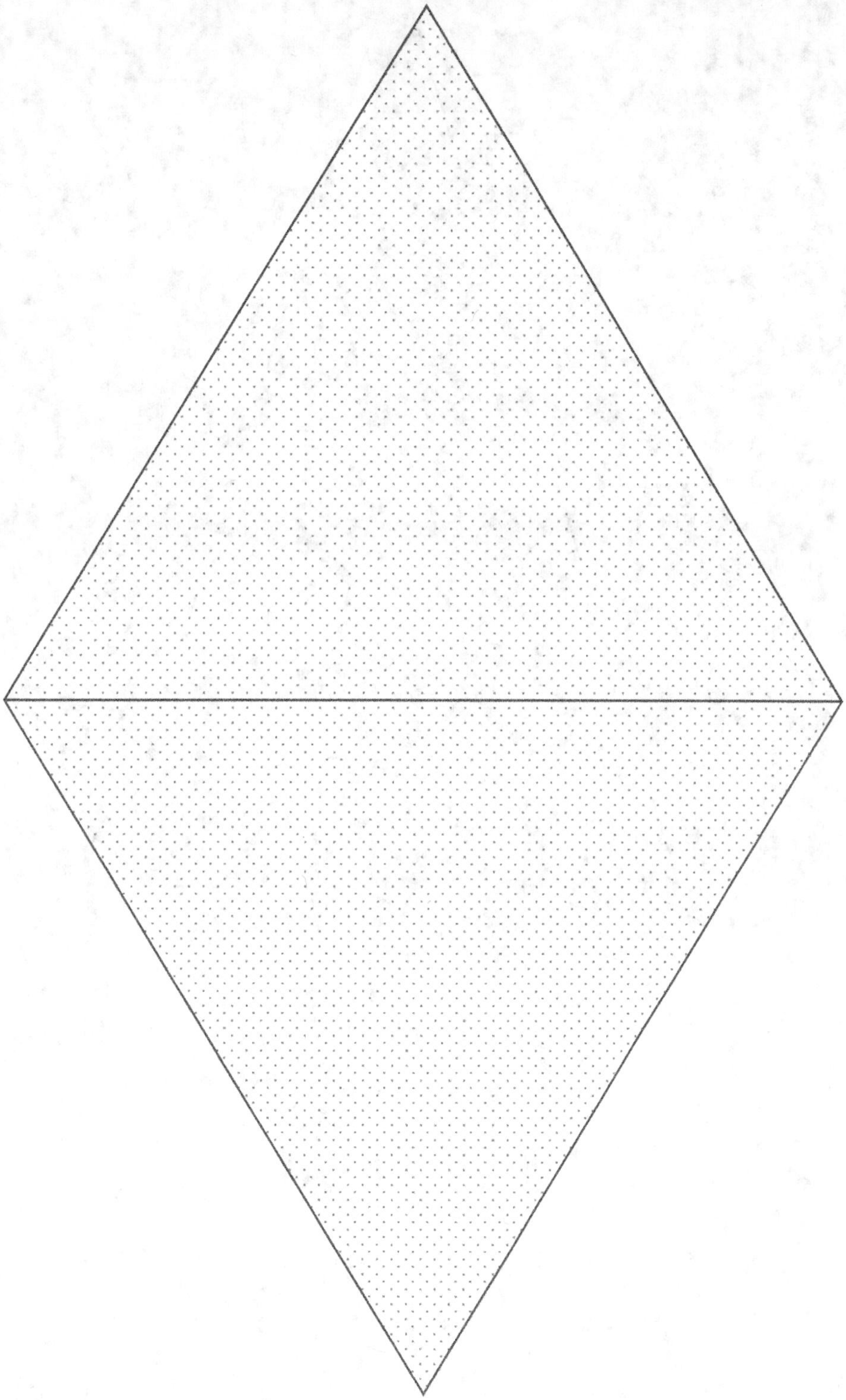

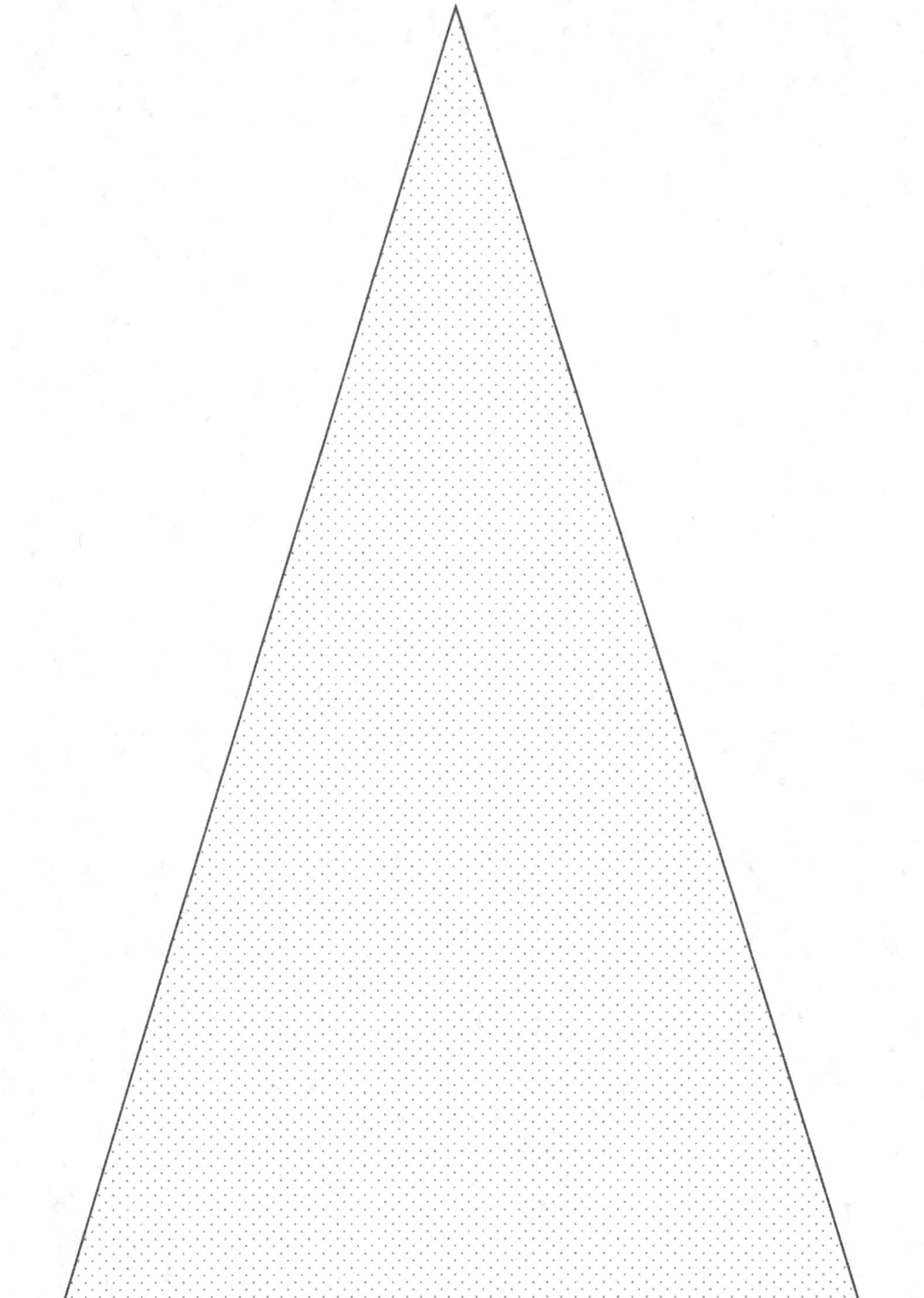

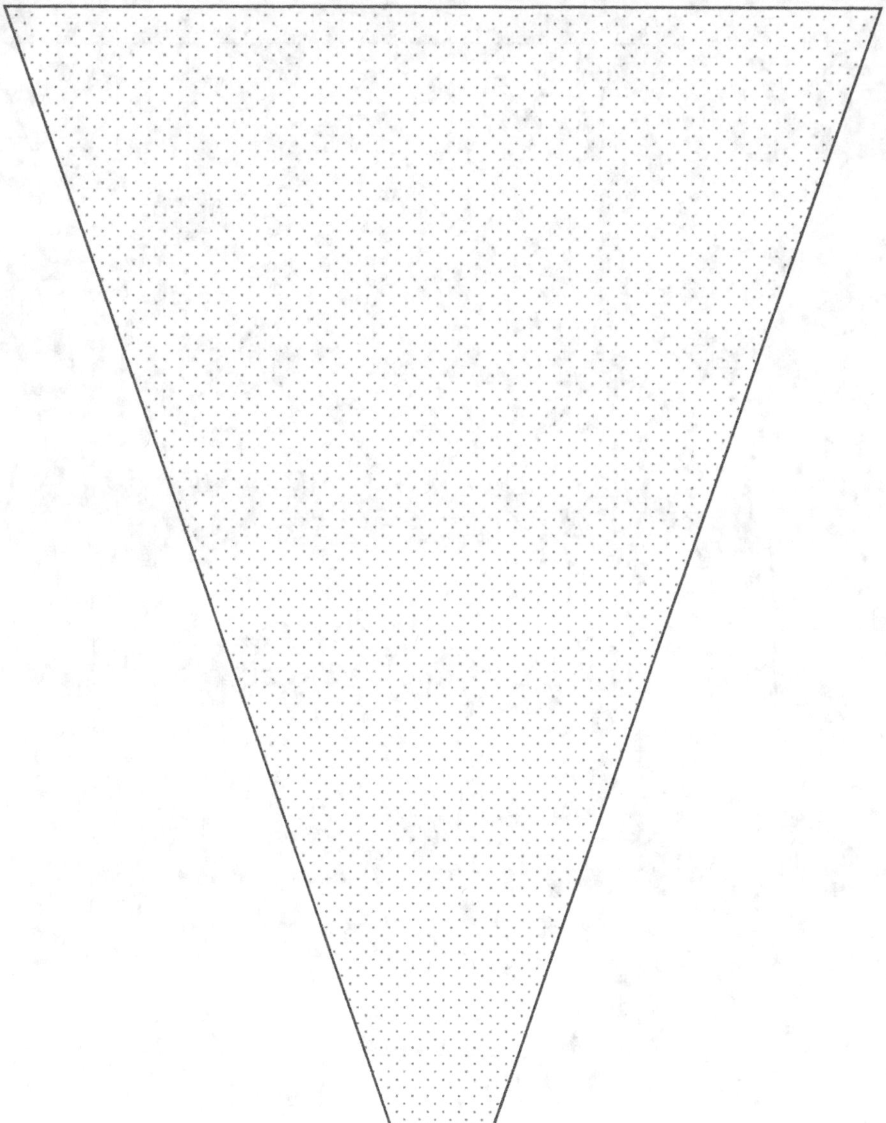

Q

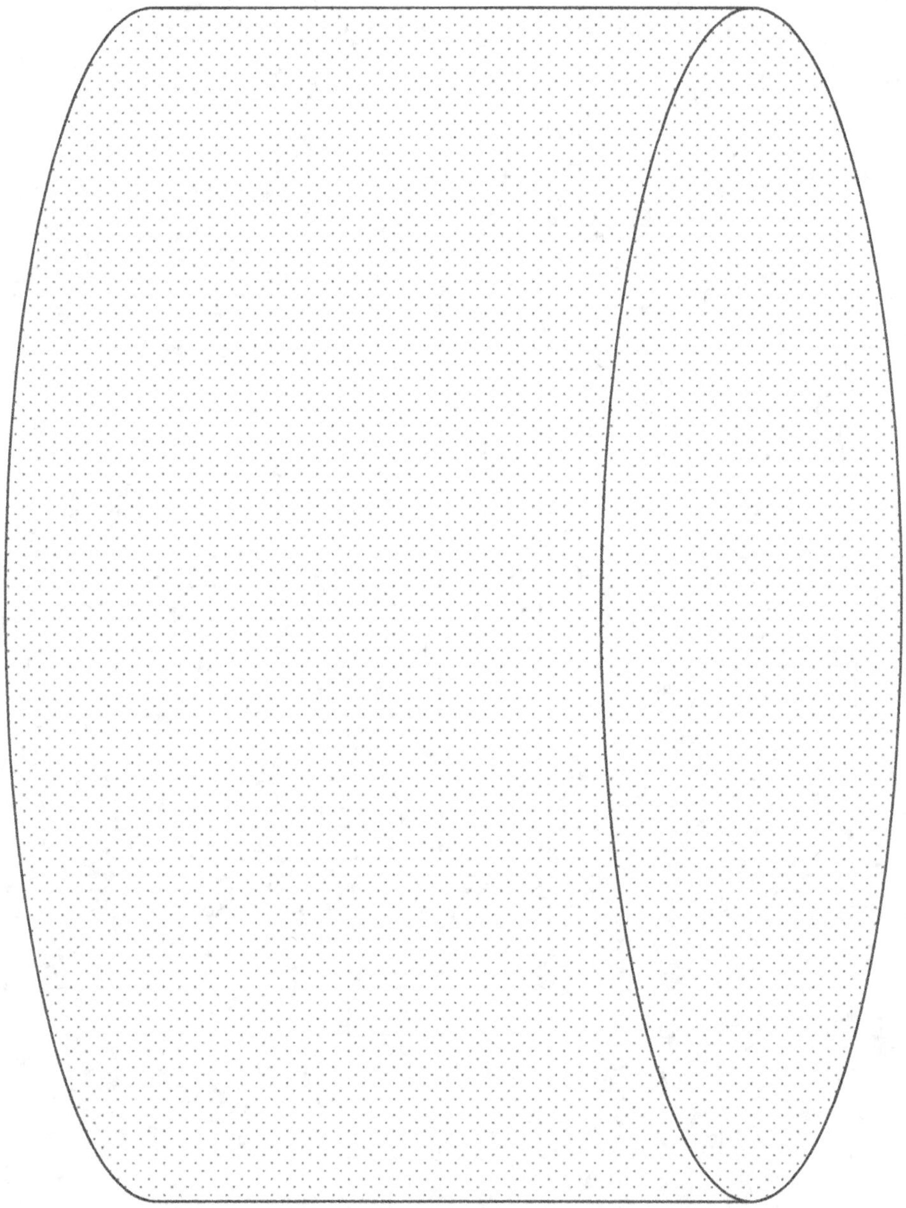

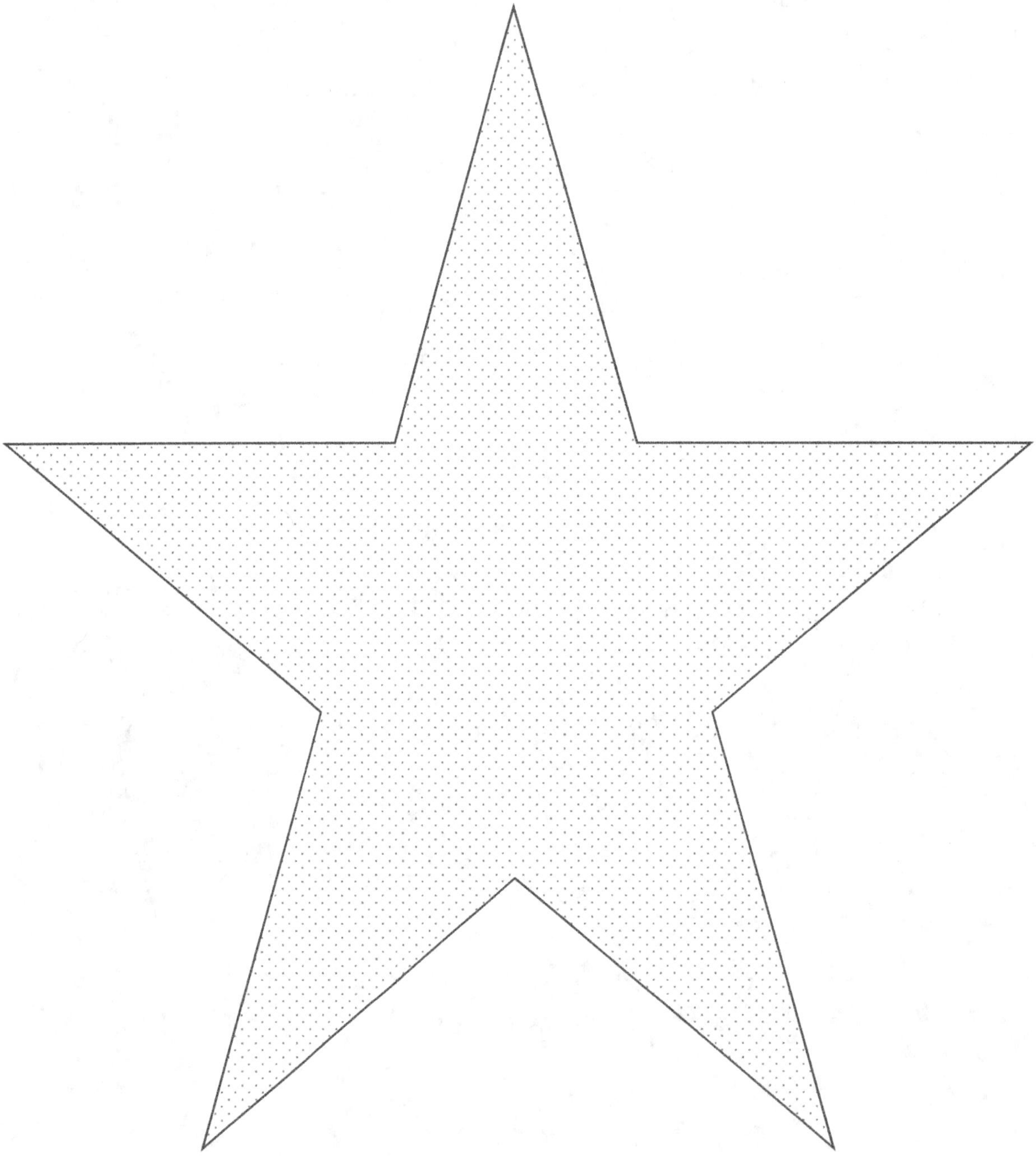

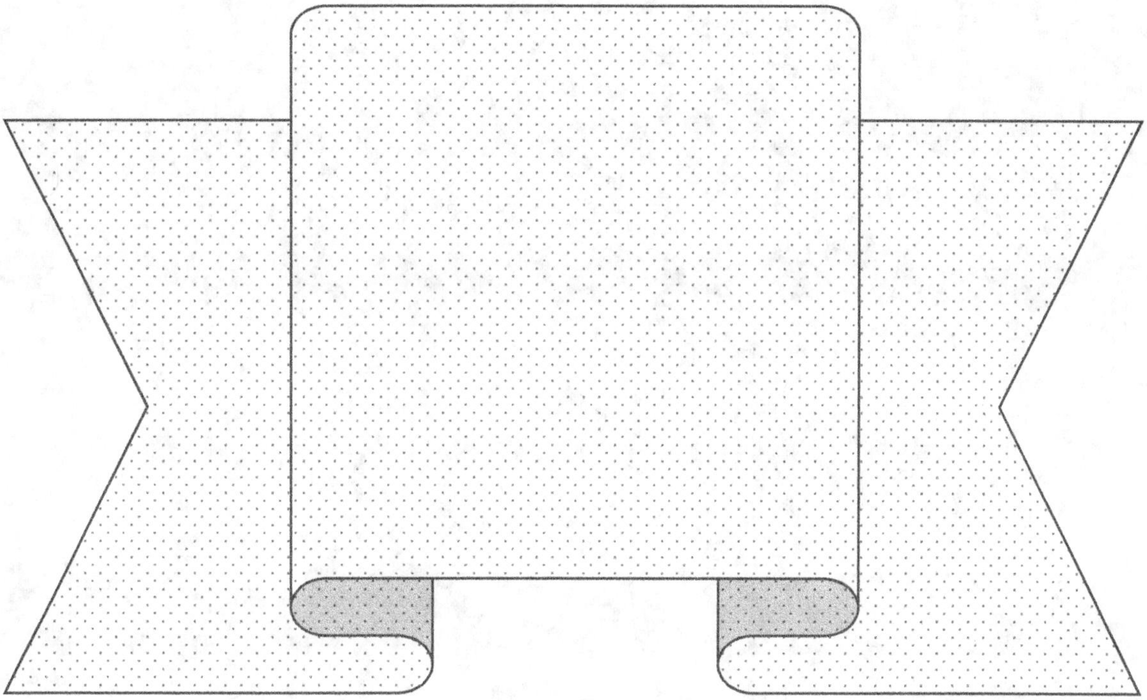

www.ingramcontent.com/pod-product-compliance
Lightning Source LLC
Chambersburg PA
CBHW081344160726
48000CB00010B/3227
* 9 7 9 8 6 7 0 3 4 3 1 7 6 *